*TWAYNE'S WORLD AUTHORS SERIES*

*A Survey of the World's Literature*

Sylvia E. Bowman, Indiana University

GENERAL EDITOR

# GERMANY

Ulrich Weisstein, Indiana University

EDITOR

*German Expressionist Drama*

*TWAS 421*

# GERMAN
# EXPRESSIONIST
# DRAMA

### By J. M. RITCHIE
*University of Sheffield*

## TWAYNE PUBLISHERS
### A DIVISION OF G. K. HALL & CO., BOSTON

**Library of Congress Cataloging in Publication Data**

Ritchie, James MacPherson, 1927–
 German expressionist drama.

 Twayne's world authors series ; TWAS 421 : Germany)
 Bibliography: pp. 185–89.
 Includes index.
 1. German drama—20th century—History and criticism.
2. Expressionism. I. Title.
PT668.R5 1977 832′.8′091 76–46324
ISBN 0–8057–6261–2

# *Contents*

# About the Author

J. M. Ritchie trained as an interpreter with the R.A.F. and later graduated from Aberdeen University with First Class Honours in modern languages and was awarded the Senatus Gold Medal. After Scotland he studied in Germany and took his doctorate at the University of Tübingen. After seven years at the University of Glasgow, he became head of the university department of German at the University of Newcastle, New South Wales, Australia. On his return to England he taught first in Hull before becoming Professor and Head of the Department of Germanic Languages at Sheffield University. He is now Pro-Vice-Chancellor of that University.

Professor Ritchie has published many articles and books on problems of German literature, mainly on Baroque, Realism and Expressionism. He has also been active as a translator. His series on German Expressionist Drama in translation published in several volumes by Calder and Boyars, London, is now complete.

# Preface

A glance at the bibliography of German Expressionist drama in translation at the end of this study will quickly show how remarkably little of it has been available in English. At one time, Toller and Kaiser did become fairly well known outside Germany, and Sternheim and Werfel also made some impact. But even for such major figures the range of available material in English was for long restricted. On the whole, pre-Expressionists like Wedekind and Strindberg became widely known and admired while the Expressionists themselves failed to penetrate beyond the frontiers of the German-speaking world. The aim of this book is therefore to promote awareness of the theatrical revolution initiated by the daring experiments of Döblin, Kokoschka, Kandinsky, Schlemmer, Schreyer, Stramm, and those who came after them. As separate volumes in this series are devoted to Kaiser, Sternheim, Werfel, Toller and Stefan Zweig, more time is spent on the little known than the known, and these giants are generally not discussed.

Like most literary and artistic movements, Expressionism is hard to define or describe in simple terms. No movement is ever the sole strand in its own time. Nevertheless, there is some justification for postulating an Age of Expressionism spanning the period from immediately before the First World War to the political, economic, social, and other complexities of the post-war period. Hence separate chapters are devoted to the war as the central experience of the age, whether in a positive or a negative sense, and to the revolution, which was also a real experience for the age, putting all the theorizing of previous generations to the test. Of course, there has been much debate, too, as to whether Expressionism is a style or a *Weltanschauung*, not least by Ulrich Weisstein in his massive symposium *Expressionism as an International Literary Phenomenon;* this line is pursued, both in the introductory chapter which discusses the antecedents of Expressionism (as well as indicating the definitive structural features of an Expressionist play) and also in sections devoted to Sorge, Hasenclever, and Lasker-Schüler. There is also a chapter devoted to specifically religious works. Despite such division into chapters, nearly all Expressionist plays could be described as lyrical, revolutionary, religious, and ecstatic. Yet, at the same time, the formalistic qualities are never lost sight of. The best way to give the uninitiated a taste of Expressionism is to offer as varied a range of examples as possible, both in the original startling German, and in translation. This is the policy adopted here. Unless otherwise stated, all translations are by the author.

I was fortunate in this study to be able to draw on a great body of critical work, and I am particularly grateful to exponents of the Expressionist revival of the caliber of Ulrich Weisstein, Horst Denkler and Walter Sokel, whose publications have helped me through "difficult" authors like Kokoschka, Kandinsky, and Stramm, or who have drawn my attention to forgotten dramatists like Brust, Jung, or Jahnn. Some of the arguments deployed in this book have been previously published by me in *Modern Drama, Seminar, Oxford German Studies*, or in the introductions to the various volumes of the German Expressionist Drama series I edited for Calder and Boyars. Such material has, however, been generally reworked and reworded. My grateful thanks also go to the Deutscher Akademischer Austauschdienst, whose financial assistance made it possible for me to spend an extended period in Marbach. The magnificence of the facilities and the helpfulness of the staff at the Literaturarchiv there are already legendary and need no special words of praise.

J. M. Ritchie

*University of Sheffield*

# Chronology

1891    Wedekind's *Frühlings Erwachen* (Spring's Awakening), published by Jean Gross in Zurich.

1892    Hauptmann, *Die Weber* (The Weavers); Maeterlinck, *Pelléas et Melisande*.

1893    Munch paints "The Scream." Lugné-Poë establishes the Théâtre de l'Oeuvre in Paris.

1895    Albert Langen publishes Wedekind's *Der Erdgeist* (Earth Spirit); Adolphe Appia's *La Mise en scène du drame Wagnérien* appears.

1896    Wedekind meets Frieda Strindberg.

1897    Birth of Wedekind's son Friedrich Strindberg.

1898    Wedekind joins the Ibsen Theater in Leipzig. In February première there of *Earth Spirit* in the Theatersaal of the Kristallpalast, with Wedekind himself as Dr. Schön.

1899    Wedekind writes his *Marquis von Keith*.

1900    Strindberg's *Dance of Death*.

1901    The Elf Scharfrichter cabaret opens in Munich. Strindberg's *Dream Play* and *The Way to Damascus I and II*. Production of Strindberg's *Easter* at the Schauspielhaus, Frankfurt. First performance of Wedekind's *Marquis von Keith*.

1902    Wedekind's *König Nicolo* (King Nicolo) published and performed.

1903    Wedekind's *Hidalla*. Shaw's *Man and Superman*. Otto Weininger's book *Geschlecht und Charakter* (Sex and Character).

1904    Strindberg's *Way to Damascus III*. First production of Wedekind's *Die Büchse der Pandora* (Pandora's Box).

1905    Gordon Craig in Berlin. Exhibition of his stage designs in Germany. Max Reinhardt takes over the Deutsches Theater. Strindberg's *Dance of Death* produced in Cologne. Wedekind's *Tod und Teufel/Totentanz* (Death and Devil/Dance of Death) written.

1906 Döblin's *Lydia und Mäxchen* (Lydia and Maxie) published, though written and produced in the previous year. Reinhardt opens the Berlin Kammerspiele with Ibsen's *Ghosts*. Reinhardt puts on Wedekind's *Spring's Awakening* with Alexander Moissi as Moritz and Wedekind as the Masked Man.

1907 Kokoschka writes *Mörder Hoffnung der Frauen* (Murderer Hope of Womankind) and *Sphinx und Strohmann* (Sphinx and Strawman), Strindberg *The Ghost Sonata*, Worringer *Abstraktion und Einfühlung* (Abstraction and Empathy).

1908 Sternheim writes *Die Hose* (The Knickers), Lautensack publishes *Der Hahnenkampf* (Cock Fight) and Wedekind *Die Zensur* (Censorship). Production of Kokoschka's *Murderer Hope of Womankind* at the Vienna *Kunstschau*.

1909 Kandinsky writes *Der gelbe Klang* (The Yellow Chord), Else Lasker-Schüler *Die Wupper*, Schönberg *Erwartung* (Expectation) and *Die glückliche Hand* (The fortunate Hand) (1909/1913).

1910 H. Walden starts his journal *Der Sturm*; publishes Kokoschka's *Murderer Hope of Womankind*. The beginnings of activism with H. Mann's essay *Geist und Tat* (Mind and Deed). Rudolf von Laban founds his school of dance in Munich. First draft of Kandinsky's *The Spiritual in Art*, published in Russian. Lautensack publishes *Dokumente der Liebesraserei* (Documents of Love's Madness).

1911 Kokoschka writes *Der brennende Dornbusch* (The Burning Bush), Fritz von Unruh *Die Offiziere* (Officers), Werfel *Der Weltfreund* (Friend to Mankind), Pfemfert starts his journal *Die Aktion*, Kandinsky and Marc found Der Blaue Reiter and put on the Blaue Reiter Exhibition in Munich. Dalcroze Institute of Dance opened in Hellerau. Sternheim's *The Knickers* has its première under the title *Der Riese* (The Giant). Lautensack's *Pfarrhauskomödie* (Vicarage Comedy) appears in print but is not performed until 1920.

1912 Strindberg dies, Barlach writes *Der tote Tag* (The Dead Day), Kaiser *Von morgens bis mitternachts* (From Morn till Midnight), and *Die Bürger von Calais* (The Burghers of Calais), Sternheim *Die Kassette* (The Strongbox) and *Schippel.* Sorge's *Der Bettler* (The Beggar) published by S. Fischer; Kandinsky and Klee publish the *Blaue Reiter Almanach*, including *The Yellow Chord*.

1913   Hasenclever writes *Der Sohn* (The Son), Carl Hauptmann *Krieg* (War), Sternheim *Snob, Kandidat* and *Perleberg*; Stramm's *Rudimentär* (Rudimentary), *Sancta Susanna, Die Unfruchtbaren* (The Unfruitful), *Erwachen* (Awakening), *Kräfte* (Forces) and *Geschehen* (Happening) are published by *Der Sturm.* Claudel produces his *L'Annonce faite à Marie* in Hellerau. Max Reinhardt produces *Schippel* at the Kammerspiele, Berlin.

1914   Schickele writes *Hans im Schnakenloch* (Jack of Midge Hole), S. Fischer publishes Kaiser's *The Burghers of Calais*, Kurt Wolff publishes Hasenclever's *The Son.* Première of Strindberg's *To Damascus* in the Lessing Theater, Berlin.

1915   Kurt Wolff publishes Werfel's version of Euripides' *Trojan Women.*

1916   Gustav Sack writes *Refraktär* (Refractory), Goering *Die Seeschlacht* (Naval Encounter), Hasenclever *Antigone*, S. Fischer publishes Kaiser's *From Morn till Midnight* and Paul Kornfeld's *Die Verführung* (The Seduction). Lautensack's *Das Gelübde* (The Vow) published in Leipzig. Première of Strindberg's *Dream Play* in Berlin and performance of Hasenclever's *The Son*, in Dresden with Ernst Deutsch in the title role.

1917   Rubiner starts to write *Die Gewaltlosen* (Those Without Violence), Kurt Wolff publishes Fritz von Unruh's *One Family.* Premières of Kaiser's *Burghers of Calais* and *From Morn till Midnight* and performances of his *Die Versuchung* (Temptation), *Der Zentaur* (The Centaur), *Die Koralle* (The Coral). Hasenclever's *Antigone* performed at the Leipzig Stadttheater.

1918   Wedekind dies. Première of Kaiser's *Gas* on November 28 at the Neues Theater in Frankfurt and the Schauspielhaus in Düsseldorf. Goll writes *Der Unsterbliche* (The Immortal) and *Der Ungestorbene* (The Undead). Hasenclever *Die Menschen* (Humanity), Becher *Ikaros*. Barlach publishes *Der arme Vetter* (The poor Cousin).

1919 Hasenclever writes *Die Retter* (The Saviors), Stefan Zweig *Jeremias* (Jeremiah), Becher his *Arbeiter Bauern Soldaten* (Workers, Peasants, Soldiers). S. Fischer publishes H. H. Jahnn's *Pastor Ephraim Magnus*. Jessner becomes Intendant of the Staatliche Schauspielhaus in Berlin and starts with an expressionistic production of Schiller's *Wilhelm Tell*. Das junge Deutschland gives a production of Lasker-Schüler's *The Wupper*; Dresden a production of Wolf's *Das bist Du* (That's You), with sets by Conrad Felixmüller; première of Toller's *Die Wandlung* (The Transfiguration). The Expressionist film emerges with *Das Kabinett des Dr Caligari* (The Cabinet of Dr. Caligari).

1920 Toller writes *Der deutsche Hinkemann* (The German Hinkemann). Werfel publishes *Spiegelmensch* (Mirror Man). Jessner produces Wedekind's *Marquis von Keith*. Première of Kaiser's *Der gerettete Alkibiades* (Alkibiades Saved), *Gas II* and of his *Europa*; première of Toller's *Masse-Mensch* (Masses and Man) in Nuremberg. Piscator opens Das Proletarische Theater in Berlin.

1921 Werfel's *Bocksgesang* (Goat Song), Carl Einstein's *Die schlimme Botschaft* (The Terrible Message), Brust's *Die Wölfe* (Wolves) appear and Franz Jung's *Kanaker* (Cannibals) and *Wie lange noch?* (How much longer?) are published by the Malik Verlag. Hindemith sets Kokoschka's *Murderer Hope of Womankind* to music. Jessner produces *Othello*.

1922 Goll's *Methusalem oder der ewige Bürger* (Methuselah or the Eternal Bourgeois) and Werfel's *Schweiger* appear. Berthold Viertel's production of Bronnen's *Vatermord* (Patricide); première of Toller's *Maschinenstürmer* (The Machine Wreckers). Brecht publishes *Baal*, based on Johst's expressionistic Grabbe play *Der Einsame* (The lonely Man). His *Trommeln in der Nacht* (Drums in the Night) is given an expressionistic first production. First American production of *From Morn till Midnight*.

1923 Bronnen and Brecht's production of Jahnn's *Pastor Ephraim Magnus*. Ernst Krenek writes his jazz opera

*Sprung über den Schatten* (Leap over the Shadow) and an operatic version of Kokoschka's *Orpheus und Eurydike* (Orpheus and Eurydice).

1924 Barlach publishes *Die Sündflut* (The Flood). Riot at Dresden opening of Toller's *Hinkemann*.

1925 Sensational première of Bronnen's *Exzesse* (Excesses). Alban Berg writes his Büchner opera *Wozzeck*, Krenek his *Jonny spielt auf* (Johnny plays the Tune).

1926 Kurt Weill's *Royal Palace* (libretto by Ivan Goll). Carl Sternheim's comedy *Die Schule von Uznach oder Neue Sachlichkeit* (The Uznach School or New Objectivity) has three simultaneous premières in Hamburg, Cologne, and Mannheim. Fritz Lang's film *Metropolis* appears.

1927 Festival of contemporary music at Baden-Baden includes Weill's *Little Mahagonny* (libretto by Brecht) and Hindemith's *Hin und Zurück* (There and Back), libretto by Marcellus Schiffer. Weill collaborates with Kaiser on *Der Zar läßt sich photographieren* (The Czar Has His Photo Taken).

1928 Weill and Brecht produce *Die Dreigroschenoper* (Threepenny Opera).

1929 Sensation over Wolf's *Cyankali* (Potassium Cyanide). Erwin Piscator's *Das politsche Theater* published. Weill and Brecht produce *Happy End*. Brecht collaborates with Hindemith in two didactic plays: *Der Lindberghflug* (The Flight over the Ocean) and *Badener Lehrstück vom Einverständnis* (Baden-Baden Cantata of Acquiescence).

1930 Wolf's *Die Matrosen von Cattaro* (The Sailors of Cattaro). Berg's Wedekind opera *Lulu*.

1933 Kaiser's *Der Silbersee* (Silver Lake) with music by Kurt Weill simultaneously in eleven cities. Nazi storm troopers interrupt the performance in Leipzig at which Weill and Kaiser are present.

# CHAPTER 1

## *Introduction*

### I  *Formal Features of Expressionist Drama*

HOWEVER disparate the views on Expressionism may be, it is generally true that an Expressionist play will tend to be different from a Neo-Romantic or Naturalistic play, no matter how extensive their common roots. Perhaps the most striking formal feature of Expressionist drama is abstraction. Essentially this means that the Expressionist dramatist is not concerned with projecting an illusion of reality on the stage; instead he gives something abstracted from reality, that is, either something taken from the real world but reduced to the bare minimum, or something totally abstracted from reality in the sense that the norms of time and place and individuation have been completely abandoned. Hence in Expressionism there is constant stress on giving the essence—the heart of the matter— deeper images instead of "mere" surface appearances. Not surprisingly, actions and plots are also pared down to the important outlines and only crucial situations are presented, while all "unnecessary" detail is eliminated. This same tendency is noticeable in the treatment of the dramatic figures, which show no characteristic features of particular individuals but tend to embody principles which the author holds to be important. As such, they bear no names and instead are often simply designated as Father, Mother, Husband, or Wife. Other dramatic figures can similarly represent states of mind, social positions, official functions, etc.; hence they are introduced merely as Cashier, Officer, and the like. The intention is clearly to move away from the specific and the conditioned to a more general sphere of reference and significance.

Abstraction of this kind is, needless to say, by no means

restricted to Expressionist drama; indeed, it is a feature of Expressionist art in general. All in all, this is in line with the Expressionists' reaction against the materialistic philosophy of the Naturalists, who tended to show the force of milieu, race, class, and social circumstance as factors conditioning the character of the individual. The Expressionists were not interested in character in this sense and did not attempt to create dramatic characters in their plays. Character for them meant a limitation of scope. They were more concerned with the soul, that which is common to all men. Instead of creating an impression of real people in real situations, the Expressionist dramatists will therefore strive with religious longing for something beyond the merely material, for eternal and transcendental values.

While this is the essential nature of Expressionistic abstraction, the rejection of the principle of mimesis was given various explanations. Kasimir Edschmid, for example, said in a speech on literary Expressionism: "The world is there. It would be senseless to repeat it." But whatever the reasons offered, time and place were ignored by the Expressionist dramatist so that he could feel free to create his own subjective universe. The dream, with its associations apparently lacking in cause or logic, was substituted for normal reality. For this practice there was a model to hand in Strindberg, though there had been forerunners within the German dramatic tradition, among whom Kleist attracted most attention. Thus, from Sorge's *Der Bettler* (The Beggar) to Kaiser's *Gas II*, one constantly encounters dreamlike sequences and figures.

After the dream, the most outstanding formal element in the Expressionist drama is the monologue. This is perhaps not surprising considering its function as the main vehicle for expressing the subjective developments within the soul of the lyrical-dramatic protagonists. The use of the monologue demonstrates yet another contrast with the Naturalists, who had argued that in real life people were supposed to converse and not soliloquize. No sooner had the monologue been banished, however, than it made its way back into the drama with even greater force than before, not least through the monologue dramas of Neo-Romantic dramatists like Hofmannsthal. The revival of the monologue was propitious for the Expressionist dramatist, who did not see life in terms of communication and sociability. Even his very explosions of longing for brotherhood and *Gemeinschaft* express an awareness of the fundamental isolation of man. Thus, egocentricity and solipsism become another hallmark of his works, expressed in formal terms by the long soliloquies of the one central figure, about whom all the other figures cluster like satellites around a major planet. The protagonist expresses *himself* alone; he does not speak for others, however much he may apostrophize mankind in general.

This solipsistic character of the Expressionist drama explains another feature, namely the scream. The Expressionist dramatist is not concerned to show normal life lived at a normal level or tempo. Instead, he strives for the exceptional and extreme situation, in which the protagonist simply explodes. In this way, once again he breaks through the restricting bonds of normalcy and is beside or beyond himself. At its best this means arriving at a state of ecstasy, which is the aim of the fundamental religious striving of the Expressionists. Ecstasy means experiencing the Divine immediately and absolutely, and not merely attempting to grasp it logically or rationally. At the same time, rhetorical and ecstatic monologues are not merely an expression of the thoughts and feelings of the isolated protagonists; they have a powerful effect on each member of the audience who is there to be stirred up out of his bourgeois mediocrity by powerful utterance. Clearly, such monologues can be as unwieldy as similar speeches in a Baroque drama by Andreas Gryphius or Daniel Caspar von Lohenstein; but the effect, once the improbability is accepted, can be equally overwhelming.

It must be admitted, however, that a potential source of weakness in Expressionist drama is the almost exclusive focus on one central protagonist, while all the other figures in the drama are reduced to mere reflections of his central position. However, it is possible to overstress the dangers of the single-perspective play. The same kind of technique was, after all, employed by Kafka in his fixed-perspective narratives to very powerful effect. At its best, as for example in Kaiser's *Von morgens bis mitternachts* (From Morn till Midnight), the solipsistic drama could be extremely successful in the way all other characters in the play mirror and reflect the problems of the cashier. Less successful is a more lyrical drama like Sorge's *The Beggar*, where even the hero's mother, father, and girlfriend seem to have been introduced simply in order to illuminate significant aspects of the young hero's soul.

As far as the actual structure of an Expressionist drama is concerned, dynamism has been singled out as the one significantly new element. By this is meant not only the forceful nature of the language employed, but also the principle whereby the protagonist is shown following a certain path through life. Hence, the drama becomes a *Stationendrama*, following the ancient religious model of the stations of the cross. This means, in effect, a sequence of scenes which follow rapidly one upon the other, often with no obvious link between them. Here again there were models in the German dramatic canon, notably in the theater of Storm and Stress, though nearer to hand were the examples of Strindberg and Wedekind. Essentially, the dynamic, episodic structure mirrored the inner turmoil and awareness of chaos in the soul of the central figure, who, following the religious model, often goes through a total transformation. Such a *Wandlung* (the title of one of Toller's plays) is most clearly apparent in the case of Kaiser's cashier who is a mere machine-man in a bank and is electrically switched on by the touch of an exotic Italian lady. Through her his transformation becomes possible; he becomes aware of "life" and tries to realize his full potential as a human being. So from being a robot he is awakened to the possibility of human existence and sets off on his quest for fulfillment, being totally transformed from one second to the next. The religious parallels to his *Aufbruch* (new start) and his pilgrimage are made symbolically clear throughout.

Even on the printed page, one major difference between an Expressionist drama and its predecessors is immediately obvious by reason of the frequent alternation between verse and prose. Here again the Expressionist sees no reason to be arbitrarily limited to the single register of natural speech and is prepared to be unnatural and poetic; not that the verse is generally poetic in the normal melodic sense: instead, the Expressionistic dramatist preferred free verse which he could move into and out of quite easily, depending on the level of speech in the particular moment of the action. In verse he was able to leave the rational, logical world behind and penetrate to the deeper levels to express the stirrings of the soul. Here the poetic utterance conforms to the ecstatic state and the elevated manner. That here the Expressionist was yet again laying himself wide open to attack from hostile critics is readily apparent. Such attacks were not slow to come and have never stopped. Yet such pathos was not a simple sign of artistic impotence; on the contrary, it was a deliberately chosen style of the large gesture and the grand manner. The scream could end in stammering incoherence; pathos could result in Baroque-like effusion; but at its best the drama could be deeply stirring in its combination of rational control and surging emotion. Here once again extreme opposites seem to be the mark of the Expressionist style, which could be extremely dense, concentrated, compressed on the one hand, while on the other this shortness, sharpness, and eruptive spontaneity could overflow into seemingly endless monologues.

It is generally easy to identify the Expressionist style on the page not merely by the alternation of verse and prose but also by the proliferation of exclamation marks, dashes, and question marks, sometimes in clusters, while even the longest speech generally breaks down into shorter units, characterized by missing articles, eliminated particles, and condensed verbal forms in order to create the lapidary style of *Ballung*. Yet while such a style is, or can be, extremely aggressive and disturbing, another feature needs to be mentioned, namely its hymnic quality. Here Sorge's *The Beggar* and Hasenclever's *Der Sohn* (The Son) offer excellent examples of the manner in which the dramatists can soar higher and higher in tone, in the manner of a musical crescendo.

And yet it must not be thought that the Expressionist always operates at such a high level; indeed, it could be argued that the most striking weapon in the Expressionist armory was the ready exploitation of the grotesque, a technique deliberately designed to effect a break from a high level of tension and plunge down to the banal. The possibilities of the grotesque had been amply demonstrated by Wedekind in *Frühlings*

*Erwachen* (Spring's Awakening) and elsewhere, and the Expressionist playwrights were not slow to follow his example. Hence, in the excitement of the Six Day Race in *From Morn till Midnight* the cashier sees five people squeezed together like five heads on one pair of shoulders till a bowler hat falls from one head onto the bosom of a lady in the audience below, to be imprinted on her bosom forever after. The bowler hat is followed by the middle man of the five, who plunges to his doom below as Kaiser puts it, like someone just "dropping" in! Such a use of the grotesque can be screamingly funny, but also screamingly terrifying. The mark of the grotesque is the distortion and exaggeration of the normal, the exploitation of caricature and distortion for effect.

## II  *The Roots of Expressionist Drama*

One question that has exercised the minds of critics is how far back one has to go to find the sources of that modernism in form and content associated with the theater of Expressionism. Medieval mystery plays have often been mentioned in this context, not merely because so many Expressionist plays share the religious striving of such early forms of theatrical production, but also because one of the features of Expressionism seems to have been a highly intellectual longing for a return to simpler forms. Hence, such obvious delight in *tableaux* as the "gothic" setting of Kaiser's *Die Bürger von Calais* (The Burghers of Calais) reveals, while the striking conclusion to Kaiser's play not only deliberately stresses the religious parallels to a secular situation, but also abandons language completely for a mode of expression relying on the visual impact of light, grouping, and gesture. Similarly, the whole play tends to follow a medieval "revue" pattern, in which sequences of scenes, or pictures, take the place of continuity of plot. Constantly referred to in connection with Expressionistic plays is the term *Stationendrama*. Hence, although an Expressionist play may appear on the surface to be very modernistic, modeled for example on Strindberg's *To Damascus*, the idea suggested is the far older one of the quest, involving the equally religious possibility of a revelation or transformation in the course of this path through

life. Little wonder, then, that Expressionistic plays often adopted
the form of the *Läuterungsdrama*, i.e., the play of purification
in which an Everyman figure experiences an illumination and
changes his life from one moment to the next. A feature of
the Naturalistic play was the depiction of man as a creature
of many conditioning factors. Man was a product of his environ-
ment, his class, race, and creed; his life ran along certain fixed
tracks from which he could not deviate. The Expressionist
dramatist, on the other hand, demonstrates that man is always
free to choose and change. His are plays of "becoming," like
Barlach's *Der blaue Boll* (Blue Boll). This character has been
forced into a certain role in society, but, as the play demonstrates, he is a man and not a machine or an animal, and in
the epic form of seven stations, or *tableaux*, he makes his
"decision." Many Expressionistic plays are therefore also *Entscheidungsdramen*, plays in which a crucial decision for the
course of a whole life is made. Very often, as in *Blue Boll*,
the decision is a fundamental one involving the "Erneuerung
des Menschen," the regeneration of man, a phrase which once
again stresses the religious nature of so many Expressionistic
works. Not surprisingly, plays of this kind tend toward universal
themes and cosmic dimensions, which may mean that the
characters are diminished, in one sense, as beings of flesh and
blood and expanded, in another, to become representative figures
for some aspect of the human dilemma.

But it would be wrong to seek the roots of Expressionist
drama exclusively in the religious drama of the Middle Ages.
Much more to the point is the general tendency to go back
beyond the comparatively recent tradition of nineteenth-century
drama to absolute simplicity combined with universal significance. This, Nietzsche had demonstrated, was to be found in
the classics, not however, in the Apollonian world of beauty
and light, but in the Dionysian sphere of darkness and ritual.
Hence, from Kokoschka's *Mörder Hoffnung der Frauen* (Murderer Hope of Womankind) onward, there is an increasing emphasis
on myth. The process of condensation and compression becomes
a paring down to the quintessential. The result is an economy
going beyond the extreme simplicity of Greek classical drama
and a concentration on all the hymnic, rhetorical potential of

language. But it must be admitted that this process of reduction and concentration, combined with ritual incantations and myth-making, has some unfortunate results. However exciting it may be, Kokoschka's playlet on the myth of the purification of man who, in his struggle with woman, dies to be reborn, is so compressed that the meaning is largely obscured. In a myth-seeking play like Unruh's *Ein Geschlecht* (One Family), which was much praised in its own time, practically every permutation in the relationship between a mother and her children is pro-jected through highly charged language—love, hate, incest, pos-sible fratricide and matricide—while the action, which is not bound to any particular age or country, takes place before a mountain cemetery high above the wars in the valley. The results of such mythologizing can often be ludicrous, as for example in the mother's dying words which sound like an echo from Kleist, whose *Penthesilea* was indeed one of the sources of Unruh's inspiration: "Here, here and there too, plunge all your steel shafts deep into my blood! I'll melt them down till nothing remains to hurt my children."

An example of the fruitful use of classical simplicity is Goering's war play *Seeschlacht* (Naval Encounter). Unruh's play is marked by shouts, screams, and exclamations, and Goering's play too is a *Schreidrama* or "scream play," another label often attached to Expressionist drama. But the striking feature of *Naval Encounter* is the tight discipline and the con-trolled, hard, highly stylized language. The quick switches from short, sharp stichomythic utterances of classical brevity to long monologues of considerable eloquence are a feature of the new Expressionist style which revels in the conjunction of extremes—ice-cold with fever-heat, compression with expansive-ness, logicality with ecstasy, stasis with dynamicism. Character-istically, too, there is little or no plot—merely the situation of men moving toward their inevitable fate, in this case sailors in a gun turret going into battle, and hence to their death. There is no realistic detail: the stylization is now complete, the compression to abstract form extreme, the process of de-personalization total. The whole work with its Socratic dialogue has the style and rigor of a classical tragedy with its constant suggestion of forces outside man controlling his destiny. Yet the final outcome is not determined by fatalism but by the individual who stands out against the forces that threaten to control him and mankind. Man's duty to man is thus the chief criterion. Hasenclever, too, adopted the classical style in his antiwar play *Antigone*; his play *Menschen* (Humanity) is an even better example of the dangers of hovering between classical simplicity and a passion-play structure.

However, Expressionist dramatists were not generally accused of excessive formalism (though, as has been seen, the tendency toward classical concentration and condensation laid them open to this charge): they were more likely to be accused of form-lessness. On the whole, this charge is probably unfair and brought about by the Expressionistic predilection for the open forms of drama associated with the German Storm and Stress. These open forms, in fact, as used by the previously under-estimated Klinger and J. M. R. Lenz, whose works included balladesque and filmic scene sequences, gradually came to be appreciated in the period which began just before World War I and ended just after it. Indeed, Lenz in particular emerged as a model for the twentieth century. An even more important influence than Lenz was Georg Büchner, also an exponent of the open form, whose most important drama was produced successfully for the first time about this period. The impact of his *Woyzeck* can be seen particularly in the Alban Berg opera *Wozzeck*, which it inspired.

## III   *Frank Wedekind and August Strindberg*

Just as the theater of German Expressionism has been classi-fied—perhaps unjustly—as a "prelude to the absurd," so too attempts have been made to establish an alternate tradition leading through Expressionism to the epic theater of Brecht. The names on this path are Lenz, Büchner, Wedekind, Stern-heim, and Brecht. Here again it is unfair to categorize dramatists who are important figures in their own right as mere stepping-stones toward a more important later development, but there can be no question of the significance of Wedekind and Stern-heim. Despite his linguistic distortions, Sternheim is very often removed from the Expressionist context because it has been felt that there is too much distance between this author of comedies and the ecstatic visionaries who are taken to be the norm. But this is surely unjust, for it is his grotesque, satiric, absurd parodying strain which increasingly seems the element of theatrical Expressionism most relevant to the present day. Be that as it may, Wedekind, his master, made the first distinct break with all preceding forms of drama and was one of the most immediate sources of the new theater. Where nineteenth-century drama had been characterized by extreme discretion, particularly in the treatment of sex, Wedekind became the man prepared to deal openly with the unspeakable; with masturbation and all the sexual fantasies of puberty in *Spring's Awakening,* and with the eternal woman and the battle of the sexes in his subsequent plays, especially *Erdgeist* (Earth Spirit) and *Büchse der Pandora* (Pandora's Box) whose very titles, with their echoes of Goethe and the classics, show that he too is reaching out beyond realism toward myth and universality. Lulu and her whole ambience of the circus, strong men, and the *demimonde,* culminating in Jack the Ripper, has proved one of the most enduring creations in the modern theater.

Another person of significance for German Expressionism was August Strindberg who has been called, with some justification, the real father of German Expressionist drama. In his paintings during the *Inferno* period in the mid-1890's, he tried to move beyond the world of appearances and to express an *inner* reality. This is the essence of the Expressionistic method, and when he applied it to drama the results were truly remarkable:

In the distinctly expressionistic plays, he gave free play to his plastic imagination, calling for a kaleidoscopic succession of outdoor and indoor settings, symbolic structures or props, and scenic transformations like the flower bud on the roof (in *A Dream Play*) that opens into a gigantic chrysanthemum. Music and acoustical effects acquire expressive importance in the dramatic action, and the magic of the modern stage lighting is constantly called upon to perform its wonders. Strindberg's expressionist plays, in brief, constitute *total theater* and represent an essential "retheatricalization" of the theater after its "detheatricalization" during the vogue of naturalism.[1]

Strindberg's play, *To Damascus*, with its contemporary dramatic structure of the path through life, had its première in Germany on April 27, 1914, at the Lessing Theater in Berlin. In 1916 his *Dream Play* had a successful première in Berlin at the Theater in der Königgrätzerstrasse and was performed again in 1917. The Max Reinhardt production at the Deutsches Theater in 1921 was a veritable triumph.[2] In his preface, the author had described his intention: He was attempting to reproduce the disjointed, though apparently logical, form of the dream. In this new kind of play, anything could happen and anything could seem possible, indeed, probable. Time and space would not exist. There would only be a flimsy foundation of actual events; otherwise, imagination would spin and weave in new patterns—a mixture of memories, experiences, whims, fancies, ideas, fantastic absurdities, improvisations, and original inventions. The personalities would split, double, multiply, vanish, intensify, become diffuse, disperse, then come back into focus. There would, however, be one single consciousness, exercising domination over the characters: the dreamer's. For him there would be no secrets, no inconsequences, no scruples, no laws. He would neither pronounce judgment nor exonerate; he would merely narrate.

As Strindberg puts it, dreams are most frequently filled with pain and less often with joy; hence his plays, like many Expressionist ones, are examinations of a tortured psyche. And yet the technique he describes is by no means restricted to tragic or gloomy themes. As Ivan Goll was to demonstrate in his satirical drama, *Methusalem oder der ewige Bürger* (Methusalem or the eternal bourgeois), alogic is also an intellectual form of humor and therefore the best weapon against the empty clichés which dominate modern life. In Goll's play, personalities do more than "split and multiply"; in the scene in which the student has a rendezvous with Ida the stage is divided by split lighting, and the student, played by three identical masked players, appears simultaneously as his own Ego, Superego, and Id.

But there are other important pointers to Expressionist drama in Strindberg's preface. Time and space do not exist, he claims. This is certainly a feature which marks the departure from the naturalistic limitation of dramatic action to a particular place or time. Similarly, the diminution in the importance of plot, which results in a certain apparent discontinuity, has been noted. Many later Expressionist plays are built on the weak foundation of a tale suitable for a novelette. In Kaiser's *From Morn till Midnight*, for example, the plot concerns a petty bank employee who embezzles some money and then proceeds to live it up when he mistakes a beautiful Italian woman for an exotic confidence trickster and lady of easy virtue. He simply picks up money from the bank and walks out, all of which is highly improbable to say the least. But Kaiser is not interested in creating an illusion of reality or *vraisemblance*. What he wants is a fundamental situation in which a man can walk out of one life and into another, an example of a new beginning (*Aufbruch*) and the Quest for Life, a refusal to accept anything less than the Absolute. The result, in Strindberg's words, may be "fantastic absurdities," some of which, as in Goll, can be grotesquely funny, but at the same time a bright light is focused on fundamental aspects of life in general.

The essence of the new drama, however, as Strindberg recognized, was the presence of the "single-minded consciousness" which holds the whole play together. This was certainly to become a crucial feature of Expressionist drama and the source of its strengths as well as weaknesses. When, as in Strindberg's *Dream Play* or Kaiser's *From Morn till Midnight*, this central figure is an Everyman, a Faust or a Christ-like figure capable of taking all the pains and pleasures of the modern world upon himself, a great work of art can result. Where, as in Sorge's *The Beggar* or Hasenclever's *The Son*, the protagonist is a youth or undeveloped artist, venting his immature outbursts on those who fail to appreciate him, the dangers of such self-centered, subjective, lyrical monologue drama become obvious, as all the other characters become diffuse—mere extensions of the central ego. Subjective *lyrical* drama is the least successful form of drama inspired by Strindberg; here his influence was often pernicious. Perhaps the most successful form of drama was that adumbrated by him in almost the same breath, namely *epic* drama, where he claims that "the dramatist will neither pronounce judgment nor exonerate, but merely narrate."

## IV  *Adolphe Appia and Gordon Craig*

So far the roots of the Expressionist revolution in the theater have been sought in the works of dramatists like Kleist, Lenz and Büchner, Wedekind and Strindberg; but it may well be that as great, if not greater, influence was exerted by certain scenic artists and theoreticians around the turn of the century. The most notable of these are Adolphe Appia and Gordon Craig. These two visionaries, in their separate ways, seem to have arrived at similar solutions to the theatrical problems of the age. Appia, in turn, immediately takes one back to Wagner, the concept of the *Gesamtkunstwerk* and the idea of total theater as a further source for the theater of Expressionism. Appia's theory emerged from his struggles with the problem of how to stage Wagner. His first booklet, *La Mise en scène du drame Wagnérian,* tackling (as the title indicates) the problem of stage design, was published in Paris in 1895, while a fuller German version appeared in Munich in 1899. This inconspicuous work had an enormous influence and, with the aid of hindsight, it is easy to see why. Appia's language was incredibly dense and obscure, but his illustrations of projected settings for Wagner's operas were striking in their unity and simplicity. Above all, he was concerned, as all later Expressionists were to be, with internal—not external—reality: "In order to express the inner reality underlying all phenomena the poet renounces any attempt to reproduce their fortuitous aspects; and once this act of renunciation has taken place the complete work of art arises...."[3] Instead of painting scenery to reproduce the "fortuitous aspects" of reality, Appia used light. For him light was the supreme scene-painter and interpreter, light was orchestrated, and a scene-builder. Lee Simonson has summed up the Appia legacy as follows:

Appia's first two volumes contain the germinal ideas that have sprouted, almost without exception, into the theories of modern stagecraft . . .—the necessity of visualising the mood and atmosphere of a play, the value of presentation as opposed to representation, the importance of suggestion completed in the mind of the spectator, the effectiveness of an actor stabbed by a spot-light in a great dim space, the significance of a "space stage" and the more abstract forms of scenic art.[4]

Here Simonson is talking in general terms of what Appia has contributed to modern stage design, but the most immediate influence of his ideas was clearly on the theater of German Expressionism.

Appia often appears to stand in the shadow of that other visionary of the theater, Gordon Craig. In 1914, both Appia and Craig were guests of honor at the International Theater Exhibition in Zurich, but prior to that it was Gordon Craig who had garnered all the limelight and had given the impression of being the fountainhead from whom all new ideas on the modern theater flowed. For George Bernard Shaw he was "a spoilt child in artistic Europe," and this description is not surprising, considering the monomanic way in which he pursued his goals, regardless of what was happening (or indeed could happen) in the real world of the theater.

Craig's published works on the theater were extensive, but even without examining them in detail the titles of some—*The Art of the Theater* (1905), *Towards a New Theater* (1912), *The Theater Advancing* (1919)—reveal some of the concerns which were to be vital for German Expressionism, and any study of contemporary German journals shows that Gordon Craig was avidly read and commented on in that country. Craig was a prophet leading theater back to its origins in dance, mime, gesture, color, line, rhythm. Yet, although it may have been true (as some commentators had suggested) that the drama was drowning in words, Craig did not argue that the text was to be downgraded in any way: on the contrary, according to him, poetry must be liberated from the ballast of a realistic set and spoken by the ideal actor. The first enemy was realism: thus, for example, when designing a set for Ibsen's *Rosmersholm*, he abandoned the photographic approach and stated:

Realism is only exposure whereas Art is Revelation; and therefore in the mounting of this play I have tried to avoid all Realism. . . . Let our common sense be left in the cloakroom with our umbrellas and hats. We need here our finer senses only, the living part of us. We are in Rosmersholm, a house of shadows. . . . [T]he birth of the new Theater, and its new Art, has begun.[5]

Paradoxically, the birth of the new theater and the new art was to be ushered in by a return to the old art of marionettes and masks. It meant, according to Craig, scenery and music, dancers, musicians, "every blessed or cursed thing that ever was, is or shall be in the Theater . . . if 'Theatrical.' " The latter addition was clearly crucial, for Craig's journal *Mask* later claimed to be entranced by the "theatrical," which it hoped would some day become the theatrical without quotation marks. Also venerated by him was the great Asiatic theater and all the dust and rags and the paint and dirt of the Old Theater. There were pointers in plenty to Expressionism in this creed, not least in the move outside the confines of Europe to the theater of Asia, but the concept which caused more confusion and controversy than anything else when put forward by Craig was what he called (using the German term) *Über-Marionette*. What led to the misunderstanding was the sentence: "The actor must go and in his place comes the inanimate figure—the *Über-Marionette*." For despite his advocacy of masks and marionettes Craig had no intention of dispensing with real actors and actresses; he merely wished to diminish the importance of the kind of actors who projected their own personalities, or behaved "naturally" on stage. For as far as he was concerned, no matter how good an actor might be, he can never fully succeed in translating what moves within him into external physical movement. If he were capable of doing this, he would surpass the marionette and become a super-marionette. But this can only be an ideal to strive for; in the meantime, according to Craig, one must be content with mime, movement, dance, and theatricality without quotation marks.

While Gordon Craig was widely misunderstood, especially in England, his ideas fell on extremely fertile ground in Germany, where men like Max Reinhardt were already engaged in experiments to expand the scope of the theater. Besides, ever since the days of Kleist's essay, "Über das Marionettentheater," there had been a lively interest in the esthetic problems of puppet theater and an awareness of the idealistic implications.

Moreover, the puppet theater was still very much alive in Germany. Hence not surprisingly, from Wedekind on, German intellectuals seem obsessed with puppets, marionettes, and mime. In a Wedekind play, all the characters speak, move, and behave in a strange, jerky, mechanical way. The same is true of a Sternheim play. The characters are not made of flesh and blood but are strange automata whose destinies seem controlled by strings pulled at a higher level. Goll's *Methusalem* has three figurines by George Grosz, in other words, cardboard cut-outs, or as he later puts it: "Masks; crude and grotesque like the emotions they represent."

## V  *Graphic and Plastic Arts*

Perhaps this is the point at which to remember the importance of dance and the graphic and plastic arts in the age of Expressionism. Much has been written about the symbolic significance of gesture and movement in German art and literature around the turn of the century, but it is important to realize that ten to twenty years later dance had assumed more than symbolic significance: it had become one of the great objects of cultural excitement. Equally important for an understanding of the theater of German Expressionism is an awareness of the part played by the graphic and plastic arts in the visual realization of dramatic works in the 1910's and 1920's, and here once again one may perhaps go back to Ibsen. When Lugné-Poë established the Théâtre de l'Oeuvre in Paris, he put on *Rosmersholm*, and other Ibsen plays quickly followed. By 1897 Edvard Munch had designed the settings for *Peer Gynt* and *John Gabriel Borkmann*, and, significantly, Lugné-Poë wanted *Peer Gynt* to be played in two distinct areas, a realistic setting for the realistic scenes and one unchanging "décor schema" for the philosophical or discussion scenes. Munch would have none of it; nevertheless, this is very much what happens in later Expressionist plays like Toller's *Die Wandlung* (Transfiguration). By 1907 Munch had done a setting of *Hedda Gabler*, which, from the description of the critics, seems to have impressed the audience by its atmospheric power and Expressionistic range of colors. Munch's sketches for Ibsen's *Ghosts*, with which Max Reinhardt opened his Kammerspiele, show the same expressive power in the strong red blouse of the girl and the yellow faces of the men in black suits.

More closely associated with the development of Expressionism in the German theater was Vassily Kandinsky, for whom Wagner's compositions were immediate expressions of the soul. In this Kandinsky was by no means backward-looking: on the contrary, he seems to have been very aware of contemporary creations, for example Schönberg's monodrama, *Die glückliche Hand* (The fortunate Hand). His own abstract stage composition, *Der gelbe Klang* (The Yellow Chord), is an attempt to escape from the impasse at which, as he saw it, modern theater had arrived. Drama consists of the inner experiences (soul vibrations) of the audience. From the opera comes music, from ballet the dance, while color assumes independent significance. *The Yellow Chord* is an amazing piece of work consisting of an introduction plus six "Bilder." There is more stage direction than dialogue, and the total effect is of an abstract color-film cartoon with music, which is incomplete without the responding vibrations of the audience. Needless to say, this piece was never performed in its own time, but its publication in the Blue Rider Almanac ensured maximum impact for Kandinsky's ideas.

Lothar Schreyer was another Expressionist deeply involved with the theater. After a spell as Dramaturg with the Deutsches Schauspielhaus, Hamburg, from 1911 to 1918, he became director of the Sturmbühne in 1918, then of the Kampfbühne in Hamburg from 1919 to 1921. Association with the Sturmbühne meant championing the works of August Stramm and Herwarth Walden. Schreyer produced Stramm's *Die Heidebraut* (The Bride of the Moor) and *Kräfte* (Forces) and Walden's *Sünde* (Sin). However, he was also able to further his own works, *Kindsterben* (Child Death), *Mann* (Man), and *Kreuzigung* (Crucifixion). *Man* was revived for the Berliner Festwochen of 1974. The evidence of his own productions which survives, e.g., the wood-cuts for his play, *Crucifixion*, is striking, and his writings on the period, *Erinnerungen an Sturm und Bauhaus* (Munich, 1956), have certainly helped to keep the memory of this exciting period of theatrical experimentation alive.

Not all the artists of the period were associated with *Der*

*Sturm* or the Bauhaus. Willi Baumeister, for example, began in 1919 with sets for Kaiser's *Gas*, followed by sets for Toller's *Transfiguration* in 1920. Barlach, who was an artist as well as a dramatist, had to face the problem of how his plays should be staged, and on the whole he did not approve of the abstract, non-Realistic, Expressionist style. Jessner, the Expressionist producer, visited him in Güstrow in 1921, in connection with a production of *Die echten Sedemunds* (The Genuine Sedemunds), and although Barlach took particular care to show all the actual places and the actual people he had drawn on for his play, the result, in his eyes, was a play by Jessner and not by Barlach: "... empty space, a white wall, the scream, the monumental style." This was too much for Barlach, and after that he kept away from all productions of his plays. But for the premières of *The Flood* (Stuttgart, 1924), *Blue Boll* (Stuttgart, 1926), and *Good Time* (Gera, 1929), he sketched his own sets and costumes for the designers, and, as might be expected, these prove much more earth-bound (despite the strong black line) than any purely Expressionistic design would have been.

Kokoschka is, of course, the other great artist-dramatist of the period. His first production of his first play, *Murderer Hope of Womankind*, at the Garden Theater of the Vienna Art Show of 1908 had been essentially an improvisation. However, this very improvisational quality embodied certain basic features of the coming Expressionist style—the reduction of the word, the minimal costumes and indications of time and place, combined with the addition of painted bodies and dynamic lighting. The playlet then went through various permutations, not least in its publication in *Der Sturm* with the artist's own startling line drawings. The production of 1917 starred Ernst Deutsch, one of the greatest actors of the period, and five years later it had become an opera with music by Hindemith and a stage population of fantastic masks and grotesque figures. As in the case of Schlemmer's *Triadic Ballet*, however short the text may appear on the printed page it is important to remember that this was not an insignificant little avant-garde work which critics and general public could safely ignore, but one which, from its inception, had been at the center of widespread interest, combining the talents of leading artists from various fields.

This is particularly true of the Dadaists who may also be discussed in this connection, for they never allowed themselves to be pushed to the periphery of public awareness, but instead proved unbelievably adept at utilizing the modern media of communication to make the general public aware at all times of their latest extravagances and advanced artistic experiments. It comes, therefore, as no surprise that another play by Kokoschka—*Sphinx und Strohmann* (Sphinx and Strawman)—should have been performed by the Zurich Dadaists in 1917. This Wedekind-inspired "Comedy for Automata" was then worked over and emerged, transformed from prose into poetry, with the biblical title *Job*.

One of the features of "modern" drama is that a play never reaches the final finished stage of classical art, hence the text itself tends to demonstrate the principle of constant flux. This is certainly true of *Job*, which created an enormous scandal at its performance in April, 1919. On the same program for this Sturmsoirée was an introduction by Tristan Tzara; Marinetti's manifesto *Futurist Literature* read by Hugo Ball, who also read poems by Kandinsky; Negro music and dancing, together with various other pieces of music; poems by Jakob van Hoddis; and some verses by Ehrenstein on Kokoschka. The première of Kokoschka's "Kuriosum" involved masks and scenery by Marcel Janco and had Hugo Ball and Emmy Hennings as the leading actors. Little wonder that it caused something of a stir. It may be doubted whether Dada should be so closely associated with Expressionism, and the Dadaists themselves were among the first to dissociate themselves from the movement; however, the connections were extremely close and the overlappings frequent. Before the outbreak of hostilities, Hugo Ball himself had been moved by Kandinsky's ideas to establish a "New Theater of the Future" that would combine all the arts. Paul Klee had been involved with him in discussions about this project. The war put a stop to such grand ideas, and during the war in peaceful Zurich they developed into a different kind of theater—cabaret.

## VI  *Cabaret and Music Drama*

It is fascinating that the artists of this period should have resorted to cabaret as an art form, and this not accidentally

34 GERMAN EXPRESSIONIST DRAMA

or under the pressure of war-time restrictions, but consciously, deliberately, and with full theoretical support. In Germany Kurt Hiller was the chief proponent before the war, although the same kind of development was taking place in other countries. In 1909 Hiller set up his first *literary* cabaret—the Neopathetisches Cabaret—followed by the Gnu in 1911: "There to salvoes of laughter from middle-class citizens who had wandered in by mistake and to the quick warmth of many disciples, appeals, polemics, philosophies, poetic works were read ... many an execution was carried out; a new pathos was proclaimed" (*Das junge Deutschland*, 1918).[6] The Neopathetic Cabaret had emerged from an earlier literary society called Der Neue Club. The idea and the name had been conceived by Ervin Loewenson, who also published a manifesto explaining what was meant by "Neopathos." This was further defined by Kurt Hiller in his opening speech, "Das Cabaret und die Gehirne—Salut," referring explicitly to Nietzsche:

Pathos not as the measured gesture and gait of suffering sons of the prophets, but as universal gaiety, the laughter of Pan. Hence it follows that we see nothing unworthy and ignoble about mingling the most serious items of philosophy amid songs and (cerebral) jokes: on the contrary, precisely because for us philosophy has not an academic, but a vital significance, is not just something to be taught, a job, morality or expenditure of perspiration, but—experience—it seems to us to be more appropriate for a cabaret than for a lecture-room or a learned journal. But these last words do after all sound like an attempt at justification; they move with steps as clumsy as the spirit of gravity; they do not dance confidently, like that merry intellectualism we long for. So I close my salute and open the Neopathetic Cabaret for adventures of the spirit. (*Sturm I*, 1910)[7]

In effect, the programs put on by the Neopathetic Cabaret anticipate those of Hugo Ball in the Cabaret Voltaire. Jakob van Hoddis may be remembered now as the author of the first Expressionistic poem, "Weltende," but this, like his other poems, "Variété" and "Couplets," was meant for public performance from the little stage. Georg Heym was also a popular performer, especially when he read his war poem, "Der Krieg" (1911), or recited his revolutionary portraits, "Robespierre" and "Marat," in the Munich satirists' club, Simplicissimus, a napkin on his head like a turban, with knives sticking out of it. After his death by drowning on January 16, 1912, there was a special memorial program for him at the Neopathetic Cabaret. Heym, as is well known, longed for war as a release from the stifling atmosphere of his age. When the war came it swept everybody along, even those whom one would have expected to be most openly opposed to it—Wedekind, Hugo Ball, Klabund, Toller were all carried along by the initial enthusiasm and the belief that Germany had been unfairly attacked by enemies from without and was fighting a defensive war. All were quickly disillusioned. As far as cabaret was concerned, it quickly became harmlessly patriotic inside Germany, and only in Zurich during the war was international antiwar cabaret activity possible.

Cabaret and music drama are obviously closely related, and it is Horst Denkler who raises the issue of music and Expressionist drama when discussing the Expressionist drama structure and film. Two of his examples—Goering's *Naval Encounter* and Kaiser's *Burghers of Calais*—are film-related dramas which he also finds operatic. What he does not discuss in any detail is the part which contemporary composers played in the music drama, for example, Hindemith's involvement with Kokoschka's *Murderer Hope of Womankind* and with Moholy-Nagy in his *Hin und Zurück* (There and Back); or Schönberg's involvement with the monodrama, *The Fortunate Hand.*

Music played an important part in the development of modern *Ausdruckstanz,* as has been noted in connection with Rudolf von Laban and his contemporaries; however, it must be admitted that all else pales by comparison with Alban Berg's *Wozzeck,* which has been described as the most outstanding example of Expressionism in music. The Expressionistic roots of Berg's inspiration are further indicated by the fact that for his other opera he moved on from Büchner (who had been rediscovered and revered by the Expressionists) to Wedekind, on whom he drew for his *Lulu,* written in a twelve-tone style. Thus, by the 1920's, music drama may be said to have had its roots in the strange combination of drama, opera, and cabaret which emerged among the Expressionists and in the alliance of jazz and serious music.

## VII  *Actor and Producer*

The operatic element in the theater of Expressionism is part of the theatricality of Expressionistic productions, and stress is often put on this aspect rather than on the esthetic worth of particular texts. This is perhaps partly excusable because the general aim of Expressionism was often antiliterary and anti-esthetic. Indeed, very often, as in Döblin's early farce, *Lydia und Mäxchen* (Lydia and Maxie), the theater itself became the object of the action and the producer seemed to become more important than the playwright. This may be one of the reasons why so few of the highly praised productions of the 1920's have survived, for nothing is so fragile or subject to fashion as the art of the actor and producer. Where the actor becomes supreme the importance of the author's text diminishes and in some cases disappears entirely, which is what happened in the theory and practice of William Wauer, the author of the pantomime, *Die vier Toten der Fiametta* (Fiametta's Four Dead), produced with Herwarth Walden's music in the Albert-Theater in Dresden in 1920. Wauer attacked the whole concept of the peep-show and the stage as an illusion of reality, attacked painted backdrops, and, instead, elevated the role of the actor.

Rudolph Blümner, who later made his name through the Sturm evenings he organized, and in particular by his recitations of August Stramm's poems, adopted an equally radical view of the actor, who, according to him, had to be "productive and not reproductive, creative and not merely interpretative." In his own poetry, e.g., "Ango Laina," he arrived at absolute art in which the word was abandoned and pure sound predominated:

> Uíja sagór
> Tailá tailá
> Schi oblaímono
> Gbomoloé oé oé oé
> Ango laína bobandá jo-ó
> Ango laína bobandá jo-ó
> Tailá tailá
>
> Sía ényo énya
> Lu líalo lu léiula

Lu léja léja liolefulu
Ango láina kbámyo
Ango láina nýome
Ango láina édue
Ango laina àngola
Laína na
Laina na
Lao

*Der Sturm*, xii, 1921

Spoken by himself, according to the theories of elocution which he developed in his book, *Der Geist des Kubismus und die Künste* (1921), this kind of artistry was, by all contemporary accounts, an overwhelming experience. But without Blümner's personal magnetism the magic disappears.

A similar reduction in the significance of the dramatist and playwright was outlined by Lothar Schreyer, for whom *Bühnengestaltung* became absolute. Rudolf van Laban became famous for the system which he worked out for dance notation. The same fame did not await Schreyer for the notation or *Spielgänge* in the form of graphic representations and hieroglyphs which he devised for his stage productions. Nevertheless, his theories also indicate a further stress on pantomime, light, masks, and costume, and a further diminution of the poetic word as spoken by the actor. The rediscovery of commedia dell'arte, pantomime, clowning, puppet theater, and ballet was of great importance in the revitalizing process which the theater of the age underwent, but such dereliction of the spoken word and restriction of the expressivity of the human voice seems to have been too much.

*Bühnengestaltung* was, however, essentially the domain of the men of the theater, and here the age of Expressionism did produce theorists and practitioners of genius. Indeed, very often accounts of those contemporary productions, which were sensationally successful, turn out to proceed largely from the production and not from the text which was the point of departure. Left with the text alone, the modern critic often finds it difficult to comprehend what all the excitement was about at the time. Sometimes, of course, a particular producer devoted his talents to the works of great dramatists, and then a new dramatic style and a new theatrical breakthrough became possible. This was the case with Leopold Jessner, whose "stairs," deriving probably from Craig and Appia, became for many the mark of an Expressionist production. But his presentations of Wedekind and Sternheim also indicate the new kind of impact an Expressionist play was capable of. In Jessner's production of Wedekind's *Der Marquis von Keith*, for example, the costumes were all black, while for contrast the characters wore wigs in colors ranging from bright red to green. Their faces were made up like masks and their movements were those of automata. The cut of the clothes, reinforced by lighting effects, produced strange distortions. The tempo was unnaturally fast, everything seemed to be done at the double. Instead of a ring on the doorbell there was a drum roll, and this echo from the variety stage was deliberately reinforced to give the effect of a variety number. For his 1928 production of Wedekind's *König Nicolo* (King Nicolo or Such is Life) Jessner parodied the tableau form of the street singer, *Moritat*, in the same way as Brecht did in his *Threepenny Opera*. Between the scenes, fairground music blared out as loudly and as crudely as possible. Jessner's productions of Sternheim were equally "artistic":

His figures are one-dimensional, they must not be deepened or rounded out. They merely represent this or that characteristic which they carry around like a cardboard shield and this is their entire role, to carry around these shields. The actor must therefore refrain from all ambition to represent human beings. . . .[8]

In Goll's *Methusalem* the actors actually carried cardboard shields.

Not surprisingly, numerous critics devoted themselves to the theoretical problems of the new acting. In 1917 Walter von Hollander published an article on the "Expressionismus des Schauspielers," but perhaps the most influential essay is that by Paul Kornfeld under the title, "Der beseelte und der psychologische Mensch":

Man, in drama as in all art, and like all art itself, is divorced from all the conditions of reality, from all restrictions, inhibitions and coincidences, and in parallel to his nature and being is "pathetic." And actors who present dramatic figures as these would be if they were to belong to real life are not playing theater and are not presenting art, but instead are misrepresenting themselves. It is not enough merely to imitate man—to present man. So the actor as the representative of thought, feeling and fate must free himself from reality! If he has to die on the stage, then do not let him first go to the hospital to learn how to die, nor to the bar to see how to behave when one is drunk. Let him dare to spread out his arms and at a rising point, to speak in a way he would never do in real life; let him therefore not be an imitator seeking his models in a world foreign to the actor, in short, let him not be ashamed to be acting, let him not pretend that this is not the theater or seek to create the illusion of a reality which for one thing he can never fully succeed in doing and which for another he could anyway only create on the stage if the art of drama had sunk so low as to be merely a more or less successful imitation of physical reality, saturated with either emotions or moral imperatives or aphorisms.[9]

This influential essay appeared in the first issue of the journal *Das junge Deutschland,* which also published the answers to a circular sent to drama schools on the problem of "expressionistic presentation." In his essay, Kornfeld called for a new generation of actors divorced from the ideal of external naturalness. This generation included Gertrud Eysoldt, Tilla Durieux, Fritz Kortner, Ernst Deutsch, and many others, though it was through the acting of Conrad Veidt and Werner Krauss in the cinema that the new Expressionist style made its impact on the world.

# CHAPTER 2

## Forerunners, One-acters, and Experiments: Döblin, Kokoschka, Kandinsky, Schreyer, Walden, Stramm, Goll

### I  Alfred Döblin

DÖBLIN'S one-acter, *Lydia and Maxie*, was written in 1905, produced for the first time in December of that year, published in 1906, and then produced again. A second version with a drastically altered ending was published in 1920. The important feature about this brief account of the origins of Döblin's playlet is the fact that it was immediately performed and printed in its own time. It was not a work which failed to gain recognition, but was accepted immediately for what it was, namely a theatrical parody. No great importance was attached to it, especially since Döblin developed into one of the great narrative talents of the age and showed little or no further interest in the theater until pushed into the sphere of didactic drama by Piscator after the First World War. It was Horst Denkler who in 1967 dug up this forgotten piece and put it ahead of Kokoschka's *Murderer Hope of Womankind* (1910) and Kandinsky's *The Yellow Chord* (1912) as the first real forerunner of dramatic Expressionism.

Whether such significance can really be attached to the work is debatable. For example, it has since been pointed out that theater parodies of this kind, some of which could equally well be brought in to antedate Kokoschka and Kandinsky, were by no means unusual in Germany and elsewhere at the turn of the century.[1] However, now that attention has been focused on this work it has proved not unworthy of critical analysis.

40

Louis Huguet, for example, has shown in his massive dissertation that Döblin draws heavily on Tieck, Wagner, and Strindberg, and these are certainly significant names in any search for the roots of theatrical Expressionism.[2] Since then Joris Duytschaever has extended the hunt to include Maeterlinck, whose dramatic works were also well known and ripe for parody at this time in Germany.[3] For example, the motto for Döblin's "Deep Reverence in One Act," namely: "In the case of a ruined stomach, salad in every form often has a pleasant effect," is taken as an echo of the ending of Maeterlinck's tragedy *La Princesse Maleine* (1899): "Nous allons déjeuner; y aura-t-il de la salade? Je voudrais un peu de salade. . . ." Certainly one of the main targets of this literary parody, as of much early Expressionism, is Maeterlinck's predilection for bloody and historical drama, the kind of drama which is denounced in the first part of Sorge's *The Beggar*. Equally ripe for parody was the Wagner of *The Flying Dutchman*, not to mention *Tannhäuser* and *Lohengrin*, though Gerhart Hauptmann, who had by this time moved on from bleak Naturalism to the sentimentalism of *Hanneles Himmelfahrt* (Hannele's Ascension), may equally well be the target of Döblin's scene with the sleeping beauty in the glass coffin.

At this point, it should be made clear that, as far as plot is concerned, it is difficult to reconstruct what Döblin's scenario is all about; that, apart from the normal sequence of scenes, there is also a play within a play; that the dialogue is extremely confused, and that the author himself gets into the action, while the actors step out of their roles. Needless to say, the set itself begins to move; a character steps out of a picture frame; cupboard, chair, and candelabra all begin to participate in the action; and even the Man in the Moon plays his part by breaking in the window panes and saying a few words. It is here, too, that echoes of Tieck begin to make themselves heard, though there is a difference. Tieck, for example, in his play *Der gestiefelte Kater* (Puss in Boots), had the consistent philosophy of Romantic irony behind his deliberate destruction of the illusion of reality. There is no suggestion of such an underlying esthetic in Döblin's case, though the results are very much the same; nor is there any suggestion that Döblin was striving for some kind of pre-Brechtian alienation effect, despite the deliberate incongruity between the spoken word and the manner of expression.

Thus, it would seem that although Döblin does anticipate some of the features of modern drama, this was not the direction taken by the majority of Expressionist dramas. Denkler has to look very hard indeed to detect any trace of the satirical tone of a Kaiser or a Sternheim. That he can find it may simply be because Döblin is so eclectic that there is something of everything, and hence there is almost bound to be some trace of absurd satire too. In effect, Döblin is much closer to Ivan Goll than to Sternheim or Kaiser; and Goll, as will be seen, tended more toward French Surrealism than toward the mainstream of German Expressionism.

## II  *Oskar Kokoschka*

With far more justification Kokoschka's playlet *Murderer Hope of Womankind* has been taken as the real beginning of theatrical Expressionism.[4] On April 14, 1910, it appeared in Berlin in the journal *Der Sturm*, founded by Herwarth Walden in the same year. Kokoschka, then twenty-four years old, had come from Vienna, where he already had acquired something of a name as a painter: but despite his poem, "Die träumenden Knaben," published in 1908 with his own illustrations, he was still unknown as a writer. However, through Viennese connections like Adolf Loos and Karl Kraus he had been able to make early contact with the *Sturm* circle and was even a member of the editorial team from March, 1910, until the beginning of 1911. Kokoschka's playlet, which is believed to have been written as early as 1907, is justly regarded as the first example of dramatic Expressionism. Appearing as it did, accompanied by Kokoschka's own startling line drawings, it immediately became known to a wide number of interested and appreciative readers. If some of the subscribers to *Der Sturm* found Kokoschka's play and the accompanying illustrations so horrific that they canceled their subscriptions, this only added fuel to the fire of interest that had been roused. However, publication in *Der Sturm* did not mean that Kokoschka's playlet also immediately conquered the theaters. Despite Strindberg and Reinhardt, the theaters were still not ready for such apocalyptic visions, and the play had to wait until 1917 for a full production and even then did not establish itself as a regular part of the repertoire. According to Denkler, the last Kokoschka production was in 1921 and thereafter he was only remembered as a man of the theater because of the operatic version of *Murderer Hope of Womankind* by Paul Hindemith and because of the opera by Ernst Křenek based on his later play, *Orpheus and Eurydice.*[5]

Kokoschka certainly exerted an enormous influence on the theater of his time, but his influence was due as much to the printed versions of his plays as to their actual performances. And here it must be said that Kokoschka never made it easy for his admirers. Between 1907 and 1918 he wrote four dramas, but these he subjected to such extensive amendment and alteration over the years that plays which were extremely elusive, not to say obscure, became even more so with the passage of time, even when it was possible to get hold of the texts for purposes of comparison. There are three different versions of *Sphinx and Strawman,* four different versions of *Murderer Hope of Womankind,* and two versions of *Schauspiel* (Play) or *Der brennende Dornbusch* (The Burning Bush). Only *Orpheus and Eurydice,* a very personal play, remains unchanged. As Denkler is able to show convincingly, the changes from version to version are by no means minor: on the contrary, they can sometimes be so drastic that the whole direction of the play is altered. Hence, *Sphinx and Strawman* started its theatrical life as a cabaret cuckold sketch in which the lady's name Lily seemed a deliberate allusion to Wedekind's Lulu. This "Comedy for Automata" itself had echoes of Kokoschka's own *Das getupfte Ei* (The Speckled Egg), a "mechanical play" for moving shadows made from copper sheets and painted paper which he had put on at the Cabaret Fledermaus in Vienna in 1907. *Sphinx and Strawman* then became a "curiosity" revealing the topsy-turvy world, before it was expanded into *Job.* The original man-plagued-by-woman theme became biblical and mythical in scope, embracing Adam and Eve and the beginnings of creation, though even here not without echoes of Wedekind. The first real performance of this play occurred in Dresden's Albert Theater in 1917 when the play was staged by Kokoschka together with *Murderer Hope of Womankind* and *The Burning Bush*. This was the same theater which, just one year earlier, had seen the production of Hasenclever's *The Son,* one of the first full-length Expressionist plays.

Critics have gone to some lengths in exploring the sources on which Kokoschka drew for his theatrical breakthrough. These include, of course, the scenic fantasy of Viennese and South German Baroque, alive especially in opera in the great works of the past like Mozart's *Magic Flute,* as well as in those of the present like Hofmannsthal's *Elektra.* Hofmannsthal had also recently treated the Sphinx theme in his *Oedipus und die Sphinx* (Oedipus and the Sphinx). But the Austrian theatrical tradition also meant Raimund, plus Nestroy's parodies and grotesque irony. Karl Kraus, Kokoschka's personal friend, had started the Wedekind wave in Vienna by his exemplary productions of *Spring's Awakening, Earth Spirit,* and *Pandora's Box,* supported by masterly introductory lectures and expositions, and Strindberg, too, had been successfully performed in Vienna, with modern limelight effects to reinforce the dramatist's visionary intentions. Certainly Kokoschka knew Strindberg and had read all his plays, in addition to attending productions in Vienna. Hence, not surprisingly, in addition to all the resources of the Viennese theater world into which he had been born, the Strindbergian battle of the sexes became his own fundamental and basic theme. At the same time, this Northern obsession acquires a peculiarly Austrian coloring, not least because of Kokoschka's readings in philosophy and psychology—in Sigmund Freud, of course, but more especially in Otto Weininger's sensational thesis, *Geschlecht und Charakter* (Vienna, 1903), which made a deep and lasting impression on him. What this meant in dramatic terms Kokoschka demonstrated in his tragicomic grotesque, *Sphinx and Strawman.* As Walter H. Sokel puts it: "In Kokoschka's play, the projection of psychic situations into symbolic images, an essential function of the subconscious mind, becomes action on the stage."[6] There are echoes here of both *The Interpretation of Dreams* and *Wit and Its Relation to the Unconscious;* hence, despite the tragic outcome the result is extremely funny, as metaphors and figures of speech are turned into stage images. When Job "allows his head to be turned by women," this *literally* happens on stage; and when he is deceived, he *literally* grows horns. This may mean, as Sokel says, a "feast of theatricality" and a rich harvest of stage gags, but it cannot be said that the meaning is always clear. Such obscurity is also a feature of Kokoschka's more famous *Murderer Hope of Womankind*. Schwerte has paraphrased the title in terms of Weininger's *Sex and Character* as: "*Mörder Hoffnung der Frauen*, that ought to mean, man is the sex slayer, the hope of woman who cannot find release in sex, but who is at all times ready to attack him and wound him mortally."[7] Certainly the battle of the sexes is the fundamental theme, and despite all other obscurities this does remain constant throughout all four versions, whatever else may change in the dialogue and general direction of the play. Denkler has summed up the "plot" as follows:

The action-model at the basis of all different versions can be reduced quite simply and structurally to the relationship of strike and counter-strike of ever increasing intensity: The man captures the woman and takes possession of her, the woman reacts against this, wounds the man and has him locked up; driven back to the man she opens the cage, then the man rejects her and goes, walking right over her.[8]

This closely resembles the end of *Sphinx and Strawman*, where the husband realizes that he has been deceived by his wife and will always be deceived by her; thereupon he gives up the ghost and she climbs over his body, coolly and unmoved, giving the order to clear away his mortal remains, since she can live on without him. Kokoschka's *Murderer Hope of Womankind* ends with the victorious male passing through all who stand in his way.

In what way, then, can Kokoschka's play be said to mark the beginnings of Expressionism on the stage? First of all, the author is clearly not too much worried about "meaning" in any intellectual sense. Not that his play is in any way "a prelude to the absurd"; it does have an underlying meaning, but Kokoschka prefers to present it visually, by means of color, light, movement, and choric gesture, instead of relying on the spoken word. Like so many of his contemporaries, he was more interested in cabaret, circus, and variety, in the possibilities of theatrical gags and shock effects. Hence, in a play like *Murderer Hope of Womankind*, stage directions take up as much space as actual dialogue, but not in the way that the stage directions become important and lengthy in a Naturalistic play where they tend to reflect the static nature of the drama by emphasizing the physical details of the conditioning milieu. Kokoschka's stage directions are dynamic, indicating that acrobatics, pantomime, gesture, and movement are more expressive than words. Often the actions are violent and extreme expressions of instantaneous responses and emotions. Most important of all, the play becomes visionary and this, as Georg Kaiser was to say, is the hallmark of Expressionist drama.

To a certain extent, then, it is true that Kokoschka's play set the pattern for the Expressionist drama to come. But the play is very brief and could only contain the *seeds* of future development. The form is extremely condensed—and such condensation was to be pursued further by the dramatists of the Sturm Circle—Stramm, Schreyer, and Walden himself, though they were not to be the most successful exponents of Expressionist drama, despite the intriguing nature of their experiments. The elimination of realistic detail, the exploitation of a myth-prone, dionysiac, classical antiquity, the color symbolism, the bestial responses, all these were elements which Expressionist dramatists would eagerly grasp and develop. But perhaps the most dangerous of all the paths that Kokoschka indicated was that toward the Scream Play (*Schreidrama*). This is a feature of Expressionism which subsequent critics have proved very unwilling to accept. Kokoschka's play was never intended as a portrayal of normal middle-class life lived at normal pitch. Instead, it deliberately tries to show life lived at fever pitch, allowing all the unspeakable thoughts and emotions to be given immediate expression. Extended over a dozen and a half pages, this is bearable, not to say exciting and invigorating. Extended over one hundred and fifty pages, such ecstatic utterances, screams, and rhythmical chants were soon to prove unbearable in the plays of Kokoschka's successors. But in this, as in all

his other plays, Kokoschka was to remain true to one thing—
theatricality.

## III  *Vassily Kandinsky*

One drama which certainly relies more on pantomime than
on words is *The Yellow Chord* by Vassily Kandinsky. A Russian
born in Moscow in 1866, Kandinsky studied law and economics
before turning to painting. In 1896 he made his way to Munich,
attended art school and later the Academy, became president
of the Phalanx group in 1901, and in 1909 helped found the
Neue Künstlervereinigung. As an artist, he is, however, far more
famous for his association with the group called Der blaue
Reiter, so named after the almanac planned and published
by Kandinsky with Franz Marc in 1912. Kandinsky's abstract
scenario, *The Yellow Chord*, included in this almanac (together
with a preface, "Über Bühnenkomposition"), had been written
in 1909, together with two other (as yet unpublished) abstract
dramas, *Schwarzweiss* (Black and White) and *Der grüne Klang*
(The Green Chord). The year 1909 would, therefore, seem to
mark a turning point in his career. It certainly marked a complete break with all naturalism, for by 1910 he had painted
his first abstract picture and composed the famous treatise on
nonrepresentational art, *Über das Geistige in der Kunst* (On
the Spiritual in Art), which has since often been reprinted
and acclaimed as one of the most significant manifestos of
modernism. At the outbreak of war, Kandinsky made his way
back to Russia by way of Switzerland and, after the revolution,
was entrusted with leading positions. By 1921, however, it had
become clear that the revolution had turned its face against
modernism in art, and so he made his way back to Germany,
where from 1922 till 1932 he was active in the Bauhaus in
Weimar, Dessau, and Berlin. Bauhaus meant taking an interest
in the theater once more, as he had at the time of the Blue
Rider. All in all, his career made him more of a German artist
than a Russian one, and he was certainly a central and seminal
figure for German Expressionism.

When one reads the text of *The Yellow Chord*, now like other
similar, important but elusive early dramatic pieces, made

readily available by Horst Denkler in *Einakter und kleine Dramen des Expressionismus*, one is faced with certain difficulties. First of all, it immediately becomes clear that such a scenario is not capable of legitimate production, and indeed it was never produced in Kandinsky's own lifetime, the first production being that of Jacques Polieri and Richard Mortensen in 1956. The text is extremely short, consisting, in the small format of the Reclam edition, of only ten pages including the title page and the dramatis personae. Described in the subtitle as a "composition for the stage," it consists of an introduction and six Bilder and needs a tenor and a choir off-stage plus an orchestra. The "characters" consist of Five Giants, Indeterminate Beings, a Child, a Man, People in loose clothing, and People in tights. No time or place is indicated, words and verses spoken or sung are either fragmentary or unintelligible, and the action, such as it is, consists largely of alternations of light and dark, music and silence, choir and orchestra. Colors are clearly extremely important and keep changing, often in time to the music. The singing is often without words and also lacking in feeling and deliberately wooden or mechanical. Gestures are jumpy or erratic, and there are sudden screams of ecstasy and terror. Toward the end, a dance emerges and by this time indefinable flying birdlike creatures, colored giants, etc., have given way to identifiable humans like the fat man in black with the white face or the child. Similarly, where before there had been timeless space now there are recognizable objects, a building like a chapel, a steeple with a bell and a rope pulled by the child. The puppet-like creatures of the fifth Bild suddenly give way, in the final image, to a bright yellow giant who grows and grows before assuming the position of the cross.

Not surprisingly, there have not been too many attempts to "explain" or interpret this scenario, but various commentators have pointed out its significance in dramatic terms.[9] First of all, it is clearly antinaturalistic in its avoidance of all marks of the "real" and in its stress on color, form, gesture, ritual language, music, and dance. It is even possible to view the text primarily as a deliberately constructed vacuum into which the audience can project its own responses; and yet at the same time it is clear that Kandinsky has not left his scenario completely empty, but has, for example, imposed his own color symbolism on the flux of images. In other words, the colors are by no means arbitrary. Indeed, using the color symbolism as set out in the second half of the sixth chapter of *On the Spiritual in Art*, Richard Sheppard has cracked the code as follows:

. . . white and blue are the colors of creative, transcendent spirituality. Yellow and red are the colors of natural vitality—unrestrained and restrained. Grey and black are the colors of spiritual emptiness. Brown and green are the colors of matter-of-fact stability. Once Kandinsky's color symbolism is understood in this way, *Der gelbe Klang* becomes a dramatic debate about the nature of reality and the place of man within that reality which poses three interrelated problems:

(i) Which is more real, Being or Nothingness, order or chaos?

(ii) Which is the stronger force, creative spirituality or anarchic natural vitality?

(iii) In the light of the answers to the first two questions, what hope is there for man?

This complex of questions sets *Der gelbe Klang* firmly within the context of Expressionism.[10]

Sheppard's interpretation is fairly convincing but not altogether compelling. There is, for example, no reason why his should be a better interpretation than that put forward by Lothar Schreyer in *Das Expressionistische Theater*, namely that Kandinsky's was a Utopian work, a re-enactment of the crucifixion which takes place when the world of light gives form to the world of matter. But what does make Sheppard's interpretation partly convincing is the fact that it is based on Kandinsky's theories of the "innere Klang," and is also consistent with the other works which go to make up the Blue Rider Almanac, including the pictures drawn from the whole range of the world's art history, from Chinese painting to Negro face masks, showing that the external form may be different in different ages and different races but that the inner spirit remains the same. The same basic idea about the nature of evolution and artistic creativity is to be found in Kandinsky's essay on form, Schönberg's essay on "Das Verhältnis zum Text," and Sabaneyev's essay on Scriabin's *Prometheus.* Everywhere in the Blue Rider Almanac the concepts of creation and chaos, ecstasy and release are prominent.

All this nevertheless presupposes a great deal of background awareness in the reader of *The Yellow Chord* and indicates some of the difficulties inevitably associated with abstract art of this kind. The artist has achieved his purpose when he succeeds in communicating the "inner necessity" he experiences to the spectator, when he evokes in him the same "soul vibrations." But how is this possible without some knowledge of the color code? Nevertheless, it is possible to appreciate what Kandinsky is attempting to do even without groping for "the meaning"; he is attempting a synthesis of three external elements in order to penetrate to inner values. These elements are: (1) musical tone and its movement; (2) physical-spiritual sound and its movement expressed through people and objects; (3) color tone and its movement. Missing from this synthesis, however, is the element of the word as a carrier of meaning. In Kandinsky's scenario, language is present only as one element among others. The words that are spoken, whispered, mumbled, and sung are there only to indicate certain possibilities and strike certain chords of memory and association. Such a play, therefore, attempts an enlargement in scope to become mythological and cosmic instead of social or real, but in practice this means a narrowing in scope to *certain* myths and *certain* themes. Over and over again, as in the plays of Herwarth Walden and Lothar Schreyer, such plays revolve around the crucifixion and the creation, love and death.

## IV *Lothar Schreyer and Herwarth Walden*

How can one assess the importance of a work like Kandinsky's *The Yellow Chord* other than by agreeing with Horst Denkler that its effect on the dramatists of the Expressionist generation was deep and lasting?[11] Lothar Schreyer, Kandinsky's most immediate follower, expressed this best perhaps in his *Das Expressionistische Theater,* when he claimed that Kandinsky had done for the Expressionist theater what Expressionist painting had done for art, namely discover the world of color anew, not by looking at any particular colored object, but by experiencing the abstract values of color. He experienced the expressive essence of colors as elemental phenomena and gave them back their vitality and symbolic force. Yet by the time Schreyer himself came to *Der Sturm* in 1916 an important phase in that journal's development lay behind it.[12] Walden had established the journal in 1910 and had been able to attract to it important figures of the new wave, like Oskar Kokoschka. From the start, his support of the new art of Expressionism was untiring and the range of his activities enormous. Himself a musician of considerable ability, he also wrote polemical articles on the arts and on the cultural life of the day, defended his artists from the attacks of conservative critics and propagated the New Art by exhibitions, performances of music, poetry, and drama. As far as the latter is concerned, it must be said that his own works (*Erste Liebe*, Ein Spiel mit dem Leben; *Die Beiden*, Ein Spiel mit dem Tod; *Sünde*, Ein Spiel an der Liebe; *Glaube*, Komitragödie; *Letzte Liebe*, Komitragödie; *Kind*, Tragödie; *Trieb*, Eine bürgerliche Komitragödie; *Menschen*, Tragödie) were not successful, and no attempt has been made in recent times to revive them. Indeed, even reading them is difficult enough.

When Schreyer joined the *Sturm*, the first receptive period of the journal's activities was drawing to a close and the Sturm Circle was developing into a clique with a very narrow and exclusive definition of Expressionism. For Walden, Expressionism essentially meant that there had to be a fundamental divorce between art and life, and Schreyer and others of the Sturm Circle agreed with him. Those immediately concerned at this stage (apart from Schreyer) were Blümner and Nell Walden. Later, it is true, Walden himself was to move away from this fundamental belief and join the German Communist Party, a development which was to change the character of *Der Sturm* completely, lead to divorce from his wife Nell and to a split with Lothar Schreyer. However, it is important to establish the original "Sturmkreis" position, especially as it affects Schreyer's theories of drama. Art for Schreyer was a necessity of the human condition; hence, establishment of the New Art leads directly to the emergence of a new society. Drama thereby should not be considered as mere entertainment or amusement but as a force capable of changing the world. The heart of this new concept of the drama is the VISION, and in his theoretical articles in *Der Sturm* Schreyer spends most of his time attempting to define the laws governing the expression of the vision, and in particular he deals with the problem of the WORD. "Schreyer tries to divest language of its rationalistic superstructure by liberating the individual word in order to show how it can be made to express and embody in itself the writer's cosmic experience."[13]

In his essays, Schreyer moves through the three possibilities of Cubism, Futurism, and Expressionism of the Word, arriving in the latter at the most advanced level when "the word produces a musical effect and communicates not on a rational but on an intuitive level." All this, however, is merely the theoretical groundwork leading from the Wortkunstwerk to the Bühnen-kunstwerk, and it leads him into a sphere very close to Kandinsky's theory and practice which culminates in the creation of the total work of art "not as an amalgamation of existing art-forms, but as an independent product calling on the fundamental elements of each."[14] What this meant in practice was the use of geometrical forms and pure colors to impart the inner vision. The word is abstracted from its normal context of associations and meaning, and taken out of its normal grammatical connections, leaving cultic rhythm and repetition of the individual word. The dramatist thereby makes it impossible for his work to be grasped intellectually: it must be intuited. The influence of Kokoschka and Kandinsky is clear, with perhaps some awareness of Arno Holz's linguistic experiments and of the personality and example of Stramm.

Schreyer's own productions seem to have relied on extensive drilling and training of amateur actors, which does not accord well with the spontaneous creativity he advocated in theory. His Spielgänge in which he recorded the details of each performance in a manner presaging Brecht's *Modellbücher* are works of art in their own right, especially the colored woodcuts for his *Crucifixion*. The reduction of the actor and the elevation of the producer is also indicated by masks and shields to conceal the actors. All in all, the impression that Schreyer's work leaves behind is that of an excess of theoretical argument for a theater of alogic and irrationalism, but with the controlling intellect at all times almost painfully present. Jones sees him as a *negative* example, in the sense that he freed his contemporaries from the constraints of traditional rules by seeking the basic elements of the creative process, and he sums up Sturm and Sturmtheorie as follows:

> . . . the development of definitive "Sturmtheorie" hardened into an extreme dogma that missionary zeal which had promoted artists like Kokoschka, Marc and Chagall or writers like Lasker-Schüler, Döblin and Apollinaire in pre-First World War Germany. "Sturmtheorie" refused to justify itself in generally comprehensible terms of rationality and acknowledged only that conforming to its own interpretation of the true art. Der Sturm thereby lost any semblance of what it claimed to signify, the expression of a vital force in human existence, and was condemned to become what it above all sought not to be: an interesting but irrelevant intellectual exercise.[15]

## V  *August Stramm*

But before Sturm is dismissed completely it is necessary to take a closer look at *the* poet and dramatist of the Sturm Circle, August Stramm (1874–1915). Stramm combines in his person and his work the two extremes of bourgeois success and artistic experimentation. To some extent, these two extremes come together in the style associated both with his name and with Expressionism, namely Telegrammstil, since he was, after all, a high official in the post office. Stramm was in tune with the most advanced thinking of his time, for poets and scholars alike had become increasingly aware of the inadequacy of linguistic communication; and testimonies like Hofmannsthal's famous "Brief des Lord Chandos," Marinetti's call for the destruction of syntax, Mauthner's linguistic philosophy, all make it clear that language, whether for commonplace or poetic speech, had become suspect. With Kokoschka, Walden, Schreyer, Blümner, and others this resulted in a quest for some means of dramatic communication, going beyond the mere word. With Stramm, on the other hand, critique of language resulted in a form of poetic concentration and condensation of a type associated with telegraphic communication, whereby an attempt was made to say as much as possible with as few words as possible, not, in other words, the code of the Prussian postal official, but the return to elemental, pregnant utterance. Stramm's extraordinary poems are therefore by no means merely the aberrant and eccentric experiments of an amateur litterateur: they are completely in tune with contemporary awareness of the disrupted nature of modern communication, the alienation of the individual, and the need for a new manner of expression.

What this means in terms of drama seems at first sight like an exercise in total destruction, in which very few of the accepted forms of the drama are left. Certainly the reduction of dialogue to a series of single word utterances and exclamations does not seem a fruitful advance, however pregnant and powerful Stramm may have felt his *paroles magiques* to be. If Expressionist drama is in any way a "prelude to the absurd," this would certainly seem to be one area in which the absurd is foreshadowed, for Stramm's plays become "pantomimes with spoken interjections" and their effect is often grotesque and comical.[16] This is in itself disturbing because the intention of the author seems rather to have been to create a mystic mesh of forces pointing away from the individual to the cosmic and eternal (although as with Walden and Schreyer, a return to the cosmic, mystical forces seems to develop very easily into a demonstration of the power of suppressed sexuality—*das Triebhafte*).

The theme of suppressed sexuality is treated by Stramm in his one-acter, *Sancta Susanna* (1914), a play produced at the Sturmbühne by Lothar Schreyer. The theme of the play has been described as "the sexual raging of a nun," but in fact it is more an attack by Stramm, the Catholic, against Christian insistence on chastity. The action, such as it is, takes place in a nunnery. Susanna is bombarded by reminders of sexuality from the outside world—the rustling of the trees, the song of the nightingale, and the moans of lovers. But the play operates not only with such atmospheric demonstrations of psychological forces; it also uses direct symbols, like the large spider which crawls out from behind the altar, indicating the religious repression which has made sex a taboo. There is a reminder of a previous nun who had rebelled against the laws of chastity and had been walled up alive. This is the martyr Susanna now follows, indicating that a newer, freer faith is emerging with her. The climax is marked by the grand gesture when she tears off her habit, bares her breasts, and frees her hair, declaiming: "Sister Clementa . . . I am beautiful. . . ." There then ensues a duel between the two nuns as Sister Clementa tries to drive her back into the bounds of chastity, while Susanna retorts by ripping the loincloth from the crucifix she holds in her hands and calling on *her* Savior to help her against theirs. The play ends with Susanna rising triumphant against the assembling nuns who call on her to confess and denounce her as Satan. In a recent book, Franz Norbert Mennemeier has described it as being somewhat in the Maeterlinck manner and as a "katholisches Nachtstück"; but essentially it demonstrates how one central figure is exposed to tremendous forces from the real, sensual world; how these forces invade her isolation within the ceremonial of the Church and the inherited beliefs of the past, so that she finally breaks free to make a new start.

If *Sancta Susanna* still seems stuck in the atmosphere of Neo-Romanticism, despite its new condensation and concentration, Stramm's *Rudimentär* (Rudimentary) is like a deliberate exercise in Naturalism. Again a one-acter, it now no longer projects the quaint world of the cloister, but the real world of the garret.

*Garret: window left, door right. The back wall slants from midway to the ceiling. The wall-paper hangs off in strips. Against the back wall wardrobe, bed and fireplace with little gas cooker; between fireplace and door the sink. Table with broken chair and stool in the middle; on the table scraps of food, paper and crummy plates and cutlery. In the bed under the blanket husband by the wall, the wife at the front and the baby all bundled up across the foot of the bed.*

The key to the action is given by the title "Rudimentary"—a word the husband keeps reading from a scrap of newspaper just visible under the peeling wallpaper, and which suggests that this is life reduced to the lowest possible level. Yet this is no normal Naturalistic exploration of the lower depths, for

there is no evidence of any sympathy for these people as dis-
possessed. Instead, their life is shown as consisting of naked
sex and lust for pleasure. Their language is the primitive jargon
of the unlettered, marked by the dialect forms of the big-city
proletariat, who speak ungrammatically and are incapable of
anything other than basic utterance. These people communicate
by grunts and groans, and their reactions are unexplained and
alogical. The "plot" is melodramatic in the extreme. Husband
and wife with their baby think they have nothing left and are
lying in bed waiting for death by gassing. The baby dies, but
they do not, nor does the dog. The gas has been cut off! and
the baby has died of natural causes. They come back from
the "dead" to find that they have a visitor—a driver with money.
So life begins again. No guidance is given by the author as to
how this glimpse of rudimentary existence is to be viewed. Is
this the image that the normal, comfortable middle class has
of the life of the lower classes? Is the audience supposed to
feel pity or envy for such totally amoral existence? Or should
the response be to find release in laughter at such grotesquely
comical exaggeration? The latter is probably the case.

Certainly the grotesque was to prove a continuing and powerful strain in the development of Expressionist drama. It is, for
example, much to the fore in Stramm's *Erwachen* (Awakening),
published in 1915 as number five in the *Sturm* book series. This
"Awakening" reads more like a silent film than a play, being
full of pregnant pauses, long stares, silences, and sweeping gestures. Here, as in all of Stramm's plays, the dialogue is basic,
not to say minimal, while the action is reduced so much as to
be almost nonexistent, and the characters have become simply
He, She, It, The Mob, etc. A man and a woman, who are not
married to each other, are discovered in a hotel room. The
result of this trivial commonplace situation or bourgeois drama
is a fundamental confrontation between Man and Woman, which
culminates in a cataclysmic vision of the CITY threatened by
oblivion by fire, only to be saved by water. This elemental
struggle also reveals naked passions not only in the individual
but also in the masses who react with bestial ferocity to any
impulse. As in *Sancta Susanna*, the outside world intrudes into
the action, when the wall literally breaks down, affording a

glimpse of the stars and the heavens, thereby indicating something far above the petty sphere of the bedroom.

*He* sees what is indicated by the stars, while *She* remains tied to bourgeois concepts of marital fidelity and love of her children. But though She is incapable of the higher flight and accepts the abuse of the mob as just, her sister (*It*) has eyes to see. The title, then, refers to the sister's *awakening* by Him to full womanhood in the same way perhaps as Kokoschka's woman is awakened to an awareness of full womanhood. The sister sees in him the genius, the super-man, the master-builder who has created the city out of his brain. She is awakened from an *It* to a *She.*[17]

Stramm's play finishes with the emergence of the New Man. But it must not be thought that this play was any more successful than his other dramas in communicating its message in dramatic terms. Herbert Ihering, the famous critic, gave one possible reaction in his cruel account of Lothar Schreyer's production of *Sancta Susanna* when he said: "This secret language, this megaphone art, these limbering-up exercises are not Expressionism."[18] In his review of *Kräfte* (Forces), Ihering showed that though he had no sympathy with Lothar Schreyer he had some appreciation of Stramm. That She (in *Forces*) when jolted out of her normal path by jealousy, should set her husband, his male and female friends upon each other, that she should make the man kill her husband, that would still be possible in the normal middle-class sphere of normal people with names and jobs. That this should not be shown as a developing situation but at moments of concentrated crisis produces a feeling of intensity which justifies the title *Forces*! Nevertheless, the final scene, when she pushes the woman's head down on the lips of her dead husband and then cuts off the lips that have kissed the body, Ihering finds unmotivated. Stramm, for him, was the end of a line, not a new beginning.

## VI  *Ivan Goll*

At various points in this discussion, mention has been made of Expressionism as "a prelude to the absurd." To no author does this phrase apply with greater justification than to Ivan

Goll (1891–1950), although it is doubtful whether one is justified in describing him as a German author, for according to his own description he was "a Jew by fate, born a Frenchman by chance, and made into a German by the whim of a rubber stamp." Certainly Goll was to move closer and closer to the French until he became identified more with French Surrealism than German Expressionism. Nevertheless, his earliest dramatic ventures were in German and have to be seen in the Expressionist context, no matter how prescient they may be of Ionesco's theater of the Absurd, or Artaud's theater of Cruelty. Like Döblin, Kokoschka, and many of the other radical modernists, he, too, was essentially a Romantic looking back beyond Maeterlinck and Wagner to Philipp Otto Runge and Novalis, back to a Golden Age of Humanity before its disappearance in the modern age of the machine and commercialism. In his isolation and *ennui* Goll not surprisingly wrote a *Melusine* (1922), a drama in four acts on the Romantic fairy-tale theme of the mermaid-like creature who marries an ordinary mortal (in this case, a property speculator). Not surprisingly, too, Goll wrote a *Chaplinade* (1920), a mimed silent film piece, in which Chaplin climbs out of the poster at the beginning and climbs back into it at the end, resigned to the fact that there is no room for true humanity in the modern world.

But it is for his Überdramen (Superdramas) that (as Mennemeier has claimed) Goll deserves a place among the most interesting German-language dramatists of the satirical theater of the Absurd.[19] In themselves, *Der Unsterbliche* (The Immortal One) and *Der Ungestorbene* (The Undead) [both 1918] may appear brief and trivial, but they are programmatic pieces which point in a new direction. Goll's preface to his two "Superdramas" makes this clear:

It is not the object of art to make life comfortable for the fat bourgeois so that he may nod his head: "yes, yes that's the way it is. And now let's go for a bite!" Art, insofar as it seeks to educate, to improve men, or to be in any way effective, must slay workaday man; it must frighten him as the mask frightens the child, as Euripides frightened the Athenians who staggered from the theater. Art exists to change man back into the child he was. The

simplest means to accomplish this is by the use of the grotesque—
a grotesque that does not cause laughter. The dullness and stupidity
of men are so enormous that only enormities can counteract them.
Let the new drama be enormous.[20]

Goll's own superdramas, though they contain enormities, are
not in themselves enormous—they are too short and slight for that.
   Much more important and much more extensive in scope is
his *Methusalem or the eternal Bourgeois* (1922), a satirical
drama with figurines by George Grosz. Clearly in the tradition
of Jarry's *Ubu Roi* and Apollinaire's *Les Mamelles de Tirésias,*
the preface nevertheless places it in the orbit of German Expressionism with its expressed intention to "strip away surface
reality to reveal the Truth of Being." In the play itself, which
is episodically composed of ten sequences, dialogue is reduced
to cliché, film projection reveals secret thoughts, humor comes
from the Joke Box, change of lighting takes the place of change
of scene, stuffed animals and furniture come to life; and in
the most striking scene of all the stage is divided in two by
split lighting while one character is divided in three, appearing
on stage played by three identical masked figures representing
his Ego, his Superego, and his Id. Masks are also worn at the
crazy tea-party scene, this time marking crude emotions like
Greed, Envy, and Curiosity. Goll states his intention explicitly:
"No more heroes, just people, no more characters, just naked
instincts. Quite naked. In order to know an insect you must
dissect it." But what has Goll accomplished by analyzing
Methusalem the eternal philistine? Has he destroyed him?
The answer must be no!

One senses that Goll like Sternheim and so many of the Expressionist
contemporaries who launched their massive onslaughts on the philistine secretly admired the anti-artistic anti-intellectual nonchalance
and resilience of the bourgeois. In fact, the image that probably
remains in the memory is not one of a shattered enemy but of
Methusalem contentedly farting in the face of the audience.[21]

No matter what their power, or how many seeds of future
development lie within their abbreviated compass, all the plays
so far considered seem like products of the fringe theater; and,

however capable of performance in practice and however influential among the emerging generation of Expressionist dramatists, they are essentially plays without words. The time has now come to return to the more traditional forms of theater, which, however many suggestions from these avant-garde forerunners and initiators they may have incorporated, still remained essentially servants of the spoken word. These are the plays *normally* examined in surveys of Expressionist drama.

## CHAPTER 3

# Lyrical Dramas:
# Sorge, Hasenclever, Lasker-Schüler

## I  Reinhard Johannes Sorge

REINHARD Johannes Sorge (1892–1916) wrote the play
*The Beggar* in Jena in 1911. After several alterations and
revisions it was published by S. Fischer in 1912. Next to
Kokoschka's playlet, *Murderer Hope of Womankind, The Beggar*
is generally accepted as the earliest document of Expressionism
in drama—not that this was by any means Sorge's earliest work
or that he arrived at this stage in one mighty leap. On the
contrary, other plays show him working his way through the
Ibsen style in *Das Unbekannte* (The Unknown), the Neo-
Romantic style in *Guntwar*; and even *The Beggar* shows marked
traces of the development from Neo-Romanticism, especially
in the earlier version, which, in the Critics' Scene, actually named
the playwrights of the school Sorge was now rejecting, namely,
Ernst Hardt, Eduard von Stucken, and Karl Gustav Vollmoeller.[1]
Sorge, in fact, provides a link between Neo-Romanticism and
Expressionism. His *Song of the Beggars* was actually written
just after he had read Maeterlinck's *Treasure of the Poor*.

The most striking feature of Sorge's play is its autobiographical
nature. In this it follows the example of Strindberg, whom Sorge
also admired, but like Strindberg he extends the personal and
autobiographical to give it general and even cosmic significance.
Not surprisingly, Sorge wanted to play the part of the poet-
protagonist himself (though he never did); and yet, although
the parallels with his own life are clear, the play always stresses
that this is not one individual fate that is being presented.
Sorge's father died insane; he had a friend like the one appearing in the play; he met the girl he was later to marry about this

61

time; he himself had just gone through a religious revelation in his conversion from Nietzsche worship to Roman Catholicism in the same way as the young poet too progresses from one faith to a higher one. But in every case the autobiographical elements become abstracted from reality and totally generalized. Sorge now deals with Madness, Friendship, and Love and Faith.

Hinton-Thomas has stressed the difference between Sorge's use of symbols and Neo-Romantic use.[2] The Neo-Romantics were concerned with sensual impressions, whereas the Expressionists' symbols are based upon an abstract concept and used to express an idea. The most striking example of this—color symbolism— is reminiscent of Kokoschka, Kandinsky, and especially of Strindberg's *Red Room*, when in *The Beggar* the color red is given an intellectual significance intended to express the *idea* of madness. Thus we find in the stage directions: "In front of a *red* curtain in the middle background are a table and chairs. In the left center is a stool. In the left background a door. The carpet is *red*, the curtains are *red*, the cushions are *red*. The table cloth is *red*. The son takes a *red* cloth from the end of the sofa." There are references such as "Mars is red" and "the river is red."

And yet Sorge's is not a play of color symbolism like Kandinsky's *The Yellow Chord*, nor does it strive primarily for synesthetic effects between color and music. It is rather a drama of the word, written in five acts of normal length and exploiting the possibilities of the long dramatic monologue and the lyrical outburst to the full. It may, from time to time, be difficult to grasp the full significance of these words, but they are clearly meaningful and can be studied and understood. Nor is this by any means a play which, by its structure, is unsuited for performance on the regular stage. Only the last two acts become so lyrical and so much concerned with the inward development of the protagonist that they lose all contact with the real world. Sorge himself recommended that Act V not be performed, and Sokel in his translation feels that Act IV can also be omitted "because the substance of the play is in the first three acts. No real development takes place in the remainder, which consists mostly of the Poet's monologues." He had earlier readily admitted:

Sorge's *The Beggar* not only initiated full-fledged German Expressionism, but is one of the most impressive examples of the Strindbergian
and Nietzschean influence, the musical-symphonic structure of so
many Expressionist plays, and the imaginative use of modern stage
techniques, especially the utilization of new lighting devices. In the
last particular, the great debt of Expressionism to experimental-
theater directors like Max Reinhardt is most evident.[3]

Although the play was accepted for performance by Max
Reinhardt's Deutsches Theater in 1912, it was not till after
Sorge's death, in fact not until December, 1917, that Reinhardt
staged it with Ernst Deutsch (the famous exponent of Hasenclever's *Son*) as the poet. In the five years since its publication
it had become known and admired, but it was this production
that really made it famous and which also started off the Junges
Deutschland series of productions of Expressionist plays. Contemporary reviews give some idea of its impact.[4] It was played
on a bare stage. Out of this great black space, which seemed
boundless, a spotlight picked out one man whose utter isolation
was thereby underlined. Or a room was marked only by a few
pieces of furniture, by door and window frames, by a free-
hanging picture, a garden was represented by a birch tree bathed
in blue light. So the real world was clearly enough marked by
carefully differentiated details; yet the audience was always
aware of a wider sphere. Everything moved quickly from light
to dark and dark to light. Scenes emerged and disappeared, a
café with prostitutes and fliers disintegrated, the groups being
suddenly no longer there, allowing conversations to start up
immediately at another point. The poet was seen in the world,
with his family, with his beloved, alone; but always the cosmic
intruded on the real.

As with any Expressionist play, it is almost impossible to talk
of *The Beggar* as having any plot. Certainly it would be wrong
to single out the remnants of traditional realistic drama from
the play and treat them as the most important elements, e.g.,
the two acts in the middle which develop a domestic tragedy
culminating in the son's murder of his parents. Although the
generation conflict was to become almost a *sine qua non* of Expressionist drama, and murdering one's father came to symbolize

the destruction of the old world by permitting the emergence of
a New Man, this in itself far from exhausts the true significance of the play. Looking at the text one can see how
much of himself Sorge has packed into it. From its inception
as Winterdrama it had as its subtitle "Theatralische Sendung.
Handlung in fünf Akten" (Theatrical Mission. Action in Five
Acts). This later became "Dramatische Sendung" (Dramatic
Mission). These words were also to become almost a commonplace of Expressionist drama. The poet or dramatist is always
filled with a sense of mission, and determined to impart it to
his audience. At the same time, the actual formulation used here
is a reference to yet another literary experience, for at the time
he was working on the drama Sorge was also reading Goethe's
*Wilhelm Meisters theatralische Sendung* (Wilhelm Meister's
Theatrical Mission), which had recently been rediscovered and
published. As has been mentioned, he reworked *The Beggar*
considerably before he arrived at the final shape of the printed
version. In particular, the fourth act was considerably shortened.
It was originally meant to contain an encounter between the
poet and figures from Neo-Romantic drama; this aspect was
moved to the first act, being placed in the mouths of the critics.
Now that all names have been dropped (with the exception of
that of Gerhart Hauptmann), only close reading of the text shows
the intention of the author to move away from Neo-Romanticism
to a new form of drama. Nevertheless, Richard Dehmel (one
of the rejected Neo-Romanticists) saw fit to award Sorge the
Kleist Prize for his play in 1912.

The whole of the first act, which introduces the central figure,
is a rejection of Neo-Romantic drama and a call for a new
kind of drama. Sorge is thereby proclaiming the need and
supplying the model for the new drama at one and the same
time. What he has created is Egocentric Drama, developing
the seeds already sown by Wedekind and Strindberg. The
dramatic ego or protagonist is a kind of spectrum, which becomes the focus for all events in the real world, while at the
same time revealing an inner state. All other dramatic figures
in the play are only there to reflect the inner process within
the protagonist. The result is a drama of extreme subjectivity and
also one in which the real world can be considerably dis-

torted because of the particular perspective through which
it is viewed.

Nevertheless, the distortion is not simply eccentric, not merely
one mad, artistic, or poetic way of looking at the world, which
can be rejected by the normal viewer as "untrue," or "unreal."
The unified perspective makes it possible for the outward appearance of things to be revealed, as they impinge upon the
protagonist; but their true nature can also be revealed as the
single seer penetrates through them to the real heart of the
matter. The protagonist thereby becomes not one particular
individual in one particular situation at one particular place
and time, but MAN exposed to the forces of the universe. This
is why on the stage there are no markers of time and place
as in a naturalistic play, but only one great black space from
which illuminating episodes are picked out by the light. This
is not the same as epic theater which attempts to present the
multiplicity of the modern world on the stage; what Sorge, the
Expressionist, is attempting to reveal are the eternal forces
beneath the surface of the real, hence the reduction to the
simple, the general, the essential. The protagonist is no super-
man, but a normal human being, variously described as Poet,
Son, Brother, Young Man, depending on what he represents in
each particular situation; he is never called Beggar, which is
the collective concept under which all the others are subsumed.
In view of the mission proclaimed at the beginning, it is, however, significant that he starts off as a poet and dramatist; but
even this is not a final classification—only one of the possible
phases he passes through in life.

The fundamental dramatic structure is that of the *way*,
making the protagonist into a religious seeker, a beggar or
pilgrim on a pilgrimage through life. The accent moves freely
from the mission of the poet to the religious implications of
the pilgrimage, a passage from purification to purification, and
a movement from one plane of purity to another, always striving
higher and higher without end. Thus, the external action is only
a scenic way of exemplifying this progression. At the end of
the play, the poet says to the girl: "I still see many steps before
me in the light. And many purities, I still did not walk through.
... My maiden, help me walk towards the next purity." The

verb he uses is "wandeln," which means "to walk" or "to change." This is significant, because the Expressionist play, emulating the Sorge model, becomes a play of Wandlung or transformation, the title indeed of the famous play by Toller. If the process is one of constant wandering, it is also one of constant change, so that the protagonist or central ego is always the same yet always different. It may be a source of weakness in the play from a dramatic point of view that it constantly returns to apodictic and general utterances from the same poetic seer, yet this seer should be progressing stage by stage.

Looking at *The Beggar* from the point of view of pre-Expressionist drama, one could describe Act I as exposition. It introduces the protagonist as an ambitious young writer eager for success. Yet already the new dramatic form is foreshadowed, as the normal realistic discussions between the young dramatist and his friend and the patron are interrupted by other group scenes involving newspaper readers, prostitutes, and pilots. What emerges from this structure is the fundamental isolation of the poet as one who must go his own way. Hence, the interpolated scenes are revealed as more than accidental glimpses of the normal world to which he is exposed. They also represent intellectual and social levels he has encountered and transcended. Instead of having him talk about these possible worlds, which would result in a drama of pure monologue, they are presented scenically.

Thus, the scene with the sensation-hungry newspaper readers is more than a satiric comment on the limited mentality of the typical bourgeois, though this was to become a favorite target of the Expressionist drama (as Goll's *Methusalem* and Sternheim's *Schippel*, both avid newspaper readers so amply demonstrate): these people are a reflection of a state of mind the poet has gone through. They see the theater in terms of scandal, sensation, and fame. He, too, had thought of it as a way of making a name for himself, before realizing that the theater must have a far higher goal, though at the same time being aware that this new kind of drama would exclude him from normal kinds of support and patronage, and even of performance. Similarly, the scene with the prostitutes is more than a mere foretaste of the notorious Expressionist predilection for such heroines; it reveals the falsification, desecration, and commercialization of love in modern life. The Poet's Girl, a fallen angel who already has a child out of wedlock, must emerge from this sphere to find true love with him. The third scene with the pilots, characterized by the kind of hymnic, poetic chant Brecht was later to use in his *Lindbergh Flight*, is also a reflection of the mind of the Poet, who, like the Fliers, is prepared to leave the world of the Patron behind, because the latter is only capable of "thinking in realities." Like the Flier, the Poet is prepared to fly to the heights even if this means overextending his powers. It is consistent with such a development in the poet that after he has been seen saying goodbye to his Friend, and to his Patron (thereby leaving possible worlds behind him), he should by the end of Act I declare his true mission to the girl and confirm the revelation and transformation he has already experienced.

Having left the public sphere behind, Acts II and III show the poet in the family sphere. To fulfill his mission the poet must also break these ties; indeed, he must prove himself by killing his father. However, patricide involves no more moral anguish than that felt by the parents in Stramm's *Rudimentary* when they allow their baby to die. Not only is there no discussion about the whys or wherefores of such an act, it is proclaimed directly as a good thing and something every son must do in his own way. Here the Father is a madman who asks for death, which comes therefore as a release for him. At the same time, he is shown as the counterimage of his son, a materialist who dreams of world conquest, just as the son has his own dreams of conquering the world.

From a dramatic point of view, the two acts of the family tragedy seem fairly realistic, despite the father's grotesque madness and crazy playing on his tin drum, yet even here the realistic level is broken through, for example, at the end of Act II, with its operatic apotheosis of love as a word duet between the Young Man and the Maiden, after a sequence involving three apparitions who appear "in front of the heavens on the threshold of the room." After discourse with these three figures (a man and two women), the young man abandons his egocentric plans and accepts his fate of constant transmutation upwards into ever higher circles of light.

If Act II is dominated by the dominant father-figure who must be removed, Act III culminates in a hymn of praise to the Mother, with "the voice of the son echoing brazenly from the darkness." This seems ironical because, by this time, the son has killed the suffering mother as well as the mad father by the usual stage device of mistaken glasses of poison, but no irony is intended. The mother is to be seen as the sacred symbol of the mystic forces, as indeed she tends to be seen in many another mythologizing Expressionist play, for example, in Fritz von Unruh's *One Family*.

The reality of the domestic tragedy having marked another phase in the poet's pilgrimage, the last two acts of the play become less tangible. The poet now knows that he must not think merely of self-realization, but must serve humanity by being active in the real world. In terms of the plot all this becomes faintly ludicrous because the poet now decides to take a job and move into the city. His actual job with a newspaper does not last long, and the major discussion with the girl (who works to support him) about whether she should keep her own baby or devote herself entirely to him is rather disturbing. But the text has to be read very closely to deduce, by the end, what is happening in the real world. Far more important than reality is this new acceptance by the poet that he is "condemned to the word" and must "speak in the symbols of eternity." Now he knows that the goal can never be reached and that he is a beggar and pilgrim who must be prepared for each new phase and purification.

By now, some of the main features of Expressionist drama as exemplified in Sorge's early play will have emerged. They are sources both of the play's strengths and its weaknesses, depending on how they are assessed. For example, it is possible to deplore the fact that this kind of lyrical, single-protagonist play reduces all the other characters to mere cyphers, reflections, or aspects of himself. There are, in fact, no characters in the proper sense; there is no psychology, no continuity. On the other hand, it has been argued that this structure gives the

play a unified perspective. Audiences now know not to look
for a plot with meaning or characters they can believe in.

The other difficulty of a play of this type is that, although
it may become extremely "theatrical" in its use of lighting, apparitions, visionary dream sequences, etc., it will also tend to
become less "dramatic," in the sense that there is no tension
attaching to the plot. The structure becomes loose and open-
ended; and, most of all, it relies mainly on monologues and
soliloquies. The more the action is removed from the external
world of real people to the internal world of representative
man, the more the structure of the drama will tend toward
the soliloquy. This was true of Neo-Romantic drama of the
Hofmannsthal-Maeterlinck type, and it is equally true of Sorge
and his successors. This being the case, the most important
element in the drama will be the spoken word, and this means
that the dramatist must become a virtuoso in varying his usage,
not only from prose to poetry, but within every register from
the most banal and down-to-earth to the most ecstatic and
operatic. Modern audiences are perhaps not so enthusiastic on
such word baths, but this is what Sorge (like so many of his
contemporaries) offers—cascades of words which are, part of
the time at least, exhilarating and exciting. Sorge has a message
and a mission: to make man more aware; to lift his gaze and
make him look beyond the numbing world of the city in which
he lives,—the reminder that one must be constantly ready for
the revelation, and for change, is made into a cosmic law.
Man is not subject to social or economic laws; he is a creature
placed between heaven and earth. It is not just the poet who
must express himself in "symbols of eternity": man in general
must become aware of his cosmic condition.

## II  *Walter Hasenclever*

Walter Hasenclever was born in Aachen in 1890 and died
in a French internment camp in 1940 after taking an overdose
of Veronal when he heard that German troops were marching
in. He wrote his first play, *Nirwana* (1909), as an eighteen-
year-old student at Oxford and paid to have it printed from
his winnings at poker. The work we are concerned with here,

however, is the play, *The Son*, which he started to write in 1913 and which was published in 1914 by Kurt Wolff in Leipzig. It was to become one of the greatest theatrical sensations of the Expressionist era.[5] Hasenclever was an extremely gifted dramatist and poet, and after writing the Expressionist plays, *Humanity* (1918) and *Die Retter* (The Saviors) (1919), he turned with equal success to boulevard theater of Parisian inspiration and wrote a series of dazzling and successful comedies. It was *The Son*, however, which first made his name.

This work, which is clearly autobiographical in inspiration, he enlarged in scope to make much more than his own personal story. He stylized it into the fate of all sons, a call to arms to all youth against old age. This transformation from direct self-reflection into a form of activism was brought about by the influence of Kurt Hiller, whose Berlin cabarets had proclaimed just such an activist program. Hiller was with Hasenclever in Heyst-an-der-Nordsee in 1913, as the author was working on his play, and must have guided him in the direction of a work which, while still egocentric, would aim at a revolutionary effect. This was certainly how Hasenclever later saw it, for example, in his "Manifesto to the *Son*" where he declared: "This play was written in 1913 and has the aim of changing the world. It represents the struggle through the birth of life, it is the revolt of the spirit against reality."[6] Back in Berlin, Hiller still took an interest in the genesis of the play and arranged for the writer to give readings from it at the Gnu Cabaret as soon as it was finished in the spring of 1914. This reading meant quite a breakthrough for Hasenclever. Kurt Pinthus was enthusiastic about the play and praised it in the *Schaubühne* as an "attempt at an expressionistic, exhibitive—bold youths might even say: metaphysical—drama, showing the evolution of a youthful soul in three days from being remote from the world, led, inflamed, to one who was independent, bold, lonely, whom all the heavens and hells of existence have tempered for action."[7]

In addition to the support of Pinthus, Hasenclever won a good friend in Kurt Wolff, the publisher, who arranged to have the play published in the *Weisse Blätter* and also brought it out as a book, which had gone through fifteen editions by 1922. Kurt Wolff also seems to have acted as a kind of agent for stage

performances. The play was a success and was performed in
Prague, Dresden, Vienna, Berlin, Stuttgart, Hamburg, Munich,
and elsewhere. However, as with so many theatrical successes,
it is difficult, so many years after the event, to understand why
it was so successful. Hasenclever's work does not seem particularly adventurous or revolutionary in form, for it retains
the traditional five-act structure; the language is, for the most
part, prosaic and conventional, except for occasional poetic monologues and outbursts of fiery rhetoric; and the plot is minimal,
not to say trivial.

The first act of *The Son* introduces the young man in conversation with his private teacher; the milieu is therefore that
of the rich middle class. The play seems to start as a school
tragedy with echoes of Wedekind's *Spring's Awakening*, for the
young hero, who seems rather old for such problems, has just
failed his *Abitur*, an oral test. So he rails against the school and
expresses his longing for the life from which his tyrannical
father keeps him. The household, as shown, is unusual, because
there is no mother, and the father lives elsewhere, leaving the
son alone with a teacher and a young female housekeeper. The
son has thoughts of suicide but feels that he cannot die because
he has never known life. There follows a discussion with a friend
who draws his attention to the feminine charms of the young
housekeeper. The scene between the son and the girl, as they
dine together, is filled with erotic tension.

Act II takes place in the same room the following morning
and brings a declaration of love between the girl and the son,
at the end of which they agree to spend the night together.
Then the father arrives, having been told of his son's failure, and
a violent confrontation ensues. The father rejects all pleas for
freedom and friendship and locks the son up in the house. The
friend, however, returns to release the son. Act III takes place
at a private Club for the Preservation of Joy. The son is introduced by his friend and gives a speech about his sufferings under
his oppressive father which sweeps the youthful audience off
its feet, and the act ends with the singing of the Marseillaise!
Act IV moves to a hotel room where the son has spent the night
with an attractive prostitute. The friend reappears and incites
him to new deeds. He has told the father where the son is,

thus ensuring that the father will drag his son back by force and compel the latter to kill him. To make absolutely sure of that, he hands the son a revolver. When the son is dragged away by the police, the friend mixes himself a glass of poison. The last act is mainly the final confrontation between father and son, the father holding a dog whip and the son the revolver! When the son points the gun at the father, the latter dies of a stroke! Kaiser was to proclaim "die Erneuerung des Menschen" as the central vision which his plays were meant to project. Significantly, the last words of the son, spoken to the girl, proclaim this theme of the rejuvenation or rebirth of man: "Freedom is at hand, and my heart is reborn for it."

Such a grotesque melodrama seems incredibly banal today, but in its own time it clearly struck many chords in the hearts and minds of German youth. First and foremost, of course, there was the generation problem (the father-son conflict), which had been a feature of German literature since the Hilde-brandslied; the important question is why this theme should have become so meaningful at this particular time. Kurt Wais, in his massive study of the *Vater-Sohn Motiv in der Dichtung*, points to the tremendous interest authors showed in this problem after the 1880's and traces it back to Sigmund Freud's psycho-analytical thesis of the Oedipus Complex. Certainly, the sexual undercurrent is very strong in *The Son*. At the same time, the conflict between the old and the new can take numerous forms—confessional, political, social, and moral—and be fought out in all sorts of different spheres—the school, the family, the professions, the state; but nowhere is the struggle closer and more intense than within the family. Thus, the father-son conflict had been dealt with many times before; the difference now is that everything is seen exclusively from the point of view of youth. This play, with its youthful protagonist, makes it mandatory for the audience to identify with *him*, to see and feel everything from *his* point of view. Obviously, much can always be said for the older generation; and much could be said here for the father. The son is a failure, a dropout, who thinks only of freedom and sex, but this is not how he is seen in the play. The young man seems to be leading a crusade against all that is ultraconservative, conventional, and traditional, and he wins!

The old man dies as soon as the gun is pointed at him. There is no revolution on a grand scale, and the action, in effect, revolves around an escape from the nursery; but it was enough of a symbolic gesture to enthuse the young public of the time. This is why the perspective of the young man is crucial in this play. Written one year before the outbreak of the Great War, it became, in the author's own words, "the expression of the awareness that we are all sons, or rather that all men are brothers." The first production of the play (in 1916) came right in the middle of the war, and this revolutionary feeling for the brotherhood of men must also have contributed to its success at that time.

The son, then, is the central figure, and all the other characters are reflections of his being and becoming. They are not named, but emerge merely as father, friend, girl, teacher, police officer. One or two names are, however, given in the club scene and its sequel. The son, who is twenty years old, assesses his failure to pass his examinations as the first positive step toward his liberation. Asked by his teacher what he will do, he gives the answer typical of an Expressionist dramatist:

Perhaps deliver a monologue. I must express myself to myself. You know that this fashion tends to be despised. I have never felt there was anything wrong in kneeling before my own pathos, for I know how bitterly serious both my joys and sorrows are. Since my earliest childhood I have learned to inspire the loneliness that surrounds me till it begins to speak to me in song. Even to this day I can go into the garden and conduct a symphony before this tree or that and be my own tenor. . . .

This is a description of the play that follows. The protagonist does, in fact, deliver monologues, kneel before his own pathos and express his joys and sorrows. For him, only life lived at the ecstatic heights is really living, and reality makes him embarrassed. However, he does not make his own way in life; instead he is guided, almost hypnotized, by a Mephisphelian "Friend" who simply appears almost out of nowhere. Significantly, in the first confrontation, which culminates in the father striking his son in the face, the father talks of himself as a doctor protecting his son from "the poison of our age." One is left wondering whether the friend represents something of this poison, for he seems decadent, blasé, the roué who has seen life, whereas the son is idealistic, enthusiastic, and, once away from his father, a born leader. The discussion at the mysterious club between Cherubin and the friend is not at all clear, but the behavior of the friend again seems very Mephistophelian because, Svengali-like, he "conducts" the son from behind the curtain as the latter delivers his impassioned speech. Equally in the scene with Adrienne, the cocotte, the friend plays a strange role, for he has betrayed the son to the father in order to force him to commit murder.

In effect, here again one must abandon the attempt to create a coherent plot out of this sequence of events and accept the various figures as projections of the feelings and emotions of the son and the stages in life he passes through. The friend becomes a dandy figure who has done all the things the son dreams of doing, but is left behind, presumably dead like the father, as the son passes beyond what they both represent. In the same way as the son leaves the friend behind, he also leaves the girl at the end of the play. Here, too, the young man has gone through a concentrated experience of love and what it means and is ready to move on to a different phase.

At the beginning, he is seen living in a house without a mother, but the brief appearance of the girl leads the friend to point out the significance of her presence, representing not only all the mysteries of life but also a key to freedom.

THE FRIEND: She will make your eyes to see—you fool at the locked gate. By her the bolts are flung open, and you will come to know something of the drama of the world. Have no fear; she is kind. Your mother too was a woman like her. You will be her child.

Act I, sc. v

The language here is uncomfortably reminiscent of Freud's Oedipus complex again, and the whole passage has been so interpreted, for despite the fact that there is no erotic association between the girl and the father, she can be viewed as the father's companion, placed by him in a position of authority

over the son (keeping him locked in, for example); so by
gaining her compliance and, indeed, her love, he is striking
against the father.

THE SON: What a lustful pleasure it is to deceive him! When I
kissed you yesterday in his room, how I relished this
good fortune. And the sofa we embraced on has felt
my vengeance. And the dead, scornful furniture, before
which my father would beat me has all, all seen the
miracle. I am no longer the one despised. I am becoming
a human being! Act II, sc. i

As far as the girl is concerned, she behaves in a motherly way
toward him, and in her love for him she thinks not of herself
but only of how to soothe his inflamed blood: "Don't go to any
other woman. With me you can do anything you want." So it
is his love for this girl, reciprocated by her, that gives him the
power to break down the walls that confine him and go out
into the world. But the girl is only his first initiation into the
world of love; he fails to keep his appointment with her for
their night of love and instead rushes off to what turns out to
be a club for pleasure-seekers. When next seen he is breakfasting
with Adrienne, the cocotte, after a night of love. She takes
money for love-making, as he has taken money for his speech,
that is, for performing "an act out of his childhood," though
not as an actor, because he meant what he said. He then accepts
her offer to be trained in love:

I am a beginner in love, that I am beginning to see clearly. But
the art is great, and a young man has to know something before he
can grasp the higher mathematics. I accept your proposal to teach
me! I admire you: you know far more than I do. I was so frightened
when we came up the stairs last night, past all the cheeky waiters.
We walked through the middle of life ... out of all the rooms in
this ghastly hotel burst forth streams, dark and unconscious. ...
Act IV, sc. i

But this, too, he must leave behind, for the friend gives him
a gun and the police come for him with handcuffs.
So far there has not been much in the play that can be

described as revolutionary from a literary point of view; yet there is no doubt that this is how Hasenclever intended it. Again and again his young hero raises his voice in passion against the oppressors; again and again he invites his listeners to identify with him in his struggle. For example, when he leaves the girl he says:

His whip does not reach me any more. Down below my crowd awaits me. There are fellows with guns among them. Perhaps they all feel the same as I do, in which case I shall appeal to them to free the young and noble in this world. Death to the fathers who despise us!                                                      Act II, sc. v

Subsequent speeches contain numerous powerful utterances of this kind, for example, when the son "promises to rise in force against all the dungeons of this earth," or when the friend proclaims the struggle against the father to be "the same as what a hundred years ago was vengeance against the princes. . . . In those days crowned heads exploited and enslaved their subjects, stole their money, locked their spirit in prison. Today *we* sing the Marseillaise!" What the Sturm und Drang young man wants is freedom, but not in any political sense. He wants the free development of his own personality. Yet though state and political institutions are not attacked, it is possible to argue that Hasenclever is demonstrating the development *toward* political awareness and maturity, the emergence of the New Man in that sense, but not his realization. What is demonstrated is the development of a young man from puberty through erotic fantasy to maturity, from anarchic hedonism toward higher goals.

Hasenclever was extremely fortunate. He not only crystallized the Youth Movement longings that were in the air at the beginning of the First World War, but also found the ideal actor for the crucial role of the son, and eventually the ideal producer. The première of the play took place in the Kammer-spielé of the Deutsches Landestheater in Prague on September 30, 1916. This, however, did not make much of a mark; the real sensation came only with the German première, a matinée at the Albert Theater, Dresden, on Sunday, October 8, 1916. Kurt Pinthus described the production as follows:

But in the Dresden production, a previously unknown actor from Prague, a contemporary of Hasenclever, created out of himself surprisingly, convincingly, overwhelmingly, the expressive style out of ecstatic pathos and sharp dialectics, the style which was to dominate the expressionist theater for the next ten years as the acting style: Ernst Deutsch, who on the day after the performance was as famous as the author and immediately engaged by Max Reinhardt for Berlin. He was considered the poet's twin brother on the stage; the eternally "fiery youth" type. . . .[8]

The effect was certainly stupendous, brought about not only by the intensity of the play and Deutsch's intoxicating expressivity, but also because most of the spectators thought of it as a political demonstration: in the midst of war a play against the ruling system, against bourgeois society, against authority and tradition and for freedom, however vaguely defined, and *for* humanity, with the singing of the Marseillaise at the end of Act III. The other stroke of luck was that the first public performance after the matinée in Dresden was at the Berlin Hof- und Nationaltheater on January 18, 1918. This production by Richard Weichert was expressionistic from beginning to end without a trace of the realistic family tragedy; and as a result it was yet again a sensational success. Hasenclever himself was present at this performance, put on in the last winter of the war despite the censor. He was on leave from Macedonia and just made it to the theater on time, intrigued by rumors that the production by Richard Weichert and the stage sets by Ludwig Sievert were scenically so bold that they put all previous solutions to the problems posed by this play in the shade. In fact, there was a rumor that a completely new style of production had been discovered. This was what Hasenclever and the audience experienced: a producer capable of abandoning the grand old style and moving on to the new, consistent with the message of the play. Visions were conjured up, the idea, the spiritual content of the play was revealed, modern pathos, a new will, the possibility of "absolute" theater.[9]

### III  *Else Lasker-Schüler*

The next play to be considered in this group of lyrical dramas was written by the poetess of Expressionism. Else Lasker-

Schüler (1869–1945) was born of Jewish parents and brought up in the Wupper valley in the town of Elberfeld. She was early in touch with the literary avant-garde and wrote for the leading journals of Expressionism, including *Die weissen Blätter*, *Die Aktion*, and *Der Sturm*. For some time she was married to Herwarth Walden. Altogether she fell in love very easily and was an extreme example of the bohemian coffee-house *littérateur*. Her main claim to literary fame is doubtless her lyrical poetry, which was admired by writers like Karl Kraus and Gottfried Benn. However, she also wrote two plays which are worthy of more than passing interest: *Die Wupper* (1909) and *Arthur Aronymus und seine Väter* (Arthur Aronymus and his Fathers [1932]). The latter, written long after the demise of Expressionism, is a sermon on her favorite theme of reconciliation, in this case between Jews and Christians, with visionary glimpses of the burning of the Jews that was to come about. In a third play, *Ich und Ich* (I and I), written probably around 1944 but published posthumously, she dealt even more directly with the theme of fascism.

*The Wupper* was named after the river and the district, and according to her own account, originally written in the low German dialect of the area, the so-called "Wopperdhaler Platt." First published as a book at her own expense in 1909, it evoked no echo until ten years later, when it was produced privately for the theater club Das junge Deutschland in Max Reinhardt's Deutsches Theater on April 27, 1919, under the direction of Heinz Herald with stage designs by Martin Stern and music especially composed by Friedrich Hollaender, a composer now better known for his film music and songs, e.g., for "The Blue Angel," but then deeply devoted to Lasker-Schüler's lyrical poetry. With that the play moved immediately into the sphere of Expressionist drama. This was still the case with the second production of 1927, under Leopold Jessner, in the Berlin Staatstheater, with direction by Jürgen Fehling. But the extraordinary feature about Lasker-Schüler's play is that it simply refuses to stay dead and buried. Unlike plays like *The Beggar* and *The Son*, which now seem beyond recovery, it seems to grow more alive and more "relevant" with the passing of the years, and the post-Hitler period has seen more than one sensationally successful revival. In 1958, the theater in Cologne, which had promised to put it on in the 1930's, at last fulfilled its promise, thereby evoking howls of protest from certain quarters in the church, and releasing anti-Semitic undercurrents which one had hoped were gone forever. Since then, the new Wuppertal Schauspielhaus has opened with Lasker-Schüler's play on its program alongside Brecht and Lessing. This might seem a mere act of local patriotism, as there are not so many plays of any stature dealing with the Wupper Valley; so the time has come to look at the text more closely to see how it is capable of stirring up such reactions.

Structurally Lasker-Schüler follows the traditional five-act pattern; but in effect her play consists of a sequence of Bilder or tableaux in the manner of the Expressionistic play. As for the plot, it is extremely elusive, despite the apparently naturalistic setting, alternating between the workers' quarters in the Wuppertal and the factory owner's villa. The beginning of Act I finds the old worker Wallbrecher in conversation with his grandson, Carl, who has decided not to follow the dyer's trade, but to study and become a pastor. This will enable him to look down on the workers from his lofty position in the pulpit. Just how deep his religious beliefs are is doubtful, for he seems more interested in social elevation, especially if it is combined with marrying the sensual Marta, daughter of the factory owner. Fortunately, Eduard, the son of the rich family, is deeply spiritual and encourages him in his studies, even though the mother does not. As in any Naturalistic play, the family which has risen to comfort and affluence is no happier or better for this; on the contrary, it is undermined by decadence and decay. This is demonstrated through Eduard's brother. Where Eduard is spiritual, Heinrich is sensual and given to alcoholic excess. At a fair, which joins rich and poor in merriment, he seduces the child Lieschen with sweets and champagne. The same fair is attended by Dr. von Simon, the efficient manager, and Don Juan, who actually runs the family business and is attempting to seduce Berta, the family maid. There is a hilarious scene in which Heinrich, the former officer, marshals the men as his soldiers against von Simon, the notorious seducer of working-class girls. Heinrich's triumph is short-lived, for he commits suicide once his seduction of young Lieschen becomes public knowledge, while she is sent to a house of correction. Meanwhile, Old Mother Pius, Carl's grandmother, encourages him to ask for Marta Sonntag's hand. He is turned down and in his rage starts to drink heavily with the very working-class types he had formerly despised. Eduard's attempts to save him are of no avail and in resignation he turns away to become a monk, and presumably to die young. His sister, meanwhile, is to be married to Dr. von Simon, the only man capable of saving the firm.

Summarizing the plot in this manner, however, gives a completely false impression of the play, for the information is never logically presented and, instead, must be pieced together from various hints and suggestions. Thus it is immediately apparent that this is not a social drama or family tragedy in the Gerhart Hauptmann manner; indeed, Lasker-Schüler herself made this clear when she described it as a Stadtballade, a city ballad. What she does is to conjure up atmospheric pictures from the past; for here again it is important to realize that although she talks of the city she does not mean the modern asphalt jungle. Hers is a city from an earlier age, around the turn of the century, when landscape and cityscape were one, and the relationships between master and worker were patriarchal. Lasker-Schüler clearly loves this place and these people without, however, merely painting a poetic picture of the "good old days." Her picture is poetic but also very real, showing how closely knit these people were, however separated they may have been by class, money, and social position. It is for this reason too, presumably, that, although there are echoes of political awareness in the play, these never come to the fore to make it a social—in the sense of socialistic—play. There is talk of a strike among the workers, but they are not interested. Carl tells them to kill the bosses, as they do in Russia, for then they could be the bosses; but they do not want this either. At the end of Act I, the words of the Social Democrat song, "Denn unsere Fahn ist rot" (Ours is the red flag) can be heard; but the real theme song that puts its mark on the play is the recurrent "Ach du lieber Augustin, alles ist tot."

Friedrich Koffka, writing in *Das Junge Deutschland*, interpreted *The Wupper* correctly when he refused to see it as a social drama in the ordinary sense.[10] Certainly the background must be there all the time—the audience must be constantly made aware of the regular rhythm of work, people going or coming back at the end of a shift, the howl of the steam whistles, the rattle of the wheels, the screech of the famous overhead train; but all this must simply reinforce the conviction that no social change can alter the fundamental nature of man's life in this world. Whether rich or poor, all are trapped in the same isolation and desolation, all are divorced from a true spiritual awareness, all have their longings. And despite the grinding nature of the surrounding world strange vibrations can be felt; a young girl will open her garret window and walk across the roof tops in her night dress, drawn by the moon; workers will walk past with their hands dyed different colors; and the ghostly chorus of the three drifters will come and go through the action, making their weird comments. In this way the real action becomes transparent, and the audience is encouraged to see everything in symbolic terms. This is particularly true of the Carousel in which the animals of the jungle are joined with the tame and go round and round to the music.

Where, then, in all this is there anything to give offense? Well-filled with "magic and melancholy and sublime innocence" it may be, but it must also be admitted that this is no play for Sunday School outings. While this is most immediately made apparent through the seduction of a minor by Heinrich, and the presence of Dr. von Simon, the seducer of working-class maidens, there are also the three drifters, one an exhibitionist, one a transvestite, and one a half-crazed seer; and of these Fred the Dangler (Pendelfrederech) in particular could be found offensive. And yet even here it is possible to argue (as Koffka has done) that these are symbolic as well as realistic figures. Viewed from the perspective of the Expressionist notion of "vitality," what these three figures may symbolize is the distortion of normal feelings and impulses in the world; and in this sense they are a reflection of what happens throughout this play, for here all love is barren and fruitless. The other theme that could give offense in the play is the religious one. What is shown by this Jewish dramatist is a world without God. Some of the characters at least are aware of this fact and try to satisfy their religious longings, but they, too, are thwarted: the Protestant convert turns to drink, while the new Franciscan seems doomed to an early death. But this still does not explain the Catholic reaction against this play.

What Lasker-Schüler has succeeded in conjuring up in this play is the vision of a city, and this is why the title *The Wupper* is particularly important. It is the river that winds through the whole action. One is tempted to compare this play with *The Beggar* and *The Son*, for example, and look for the person or protagonist who becomes the single perspective for the action (at first it appears to be Old Mother Pius with her quasi-magic powers, second sight and power over people). In the end, however, the real protagonist is the Wupper itself which focuses the atomized glimpses of the action. This is what makes this play into the German *Under Milk Wood*.[11] Whether one is justified in describing it as an Expressionist play is still a matter for debate; without question, however, this is how this fantastic play is best produced: the set, the music, the costumes, and the characters must all work together to create the unified vision of the poetic city:

A special rhythm of rise and fall over it all was what we had in mind. Dark transformations connect each act with the next. The always strange, scarcely noticeable change-over of gently swaying sets, the hollow role of the revolving stage, almost covered up by the accompanying, connecting music, seemed as never before appropriate for the style of this fantastic play. Curtain fall, lighted auditorium would, we felt, have hindered the continuing atmosphere, would have had a cooling effect and torn the lightly spun threads. Only after the fair, which, like a symbol of the confusion of life, stands in the middle of the play, is a stronger caesura noticeable; the curtain falls for the one and only time.[12]

## CHAPTER 4

# War: Hauptmann, Schickele, Sack, Zweig, von Unruh, Goering, Hasenclever

### Early Reactions to the War

NOT all German-speaking intellectuals were swept along by the jingoistic wave of enthusiasm. The man who emerged most clearly as the leader of the antiwar movement was René Schickele (1883–1940), whom Thomas Mann was to describe as "the tactical leader of Expressionism."[1] In January, 1915, Schickele took over *Die weissen Blätter* and guided its destinies over the next six years. The very first number had contained Max Scheler's essay on "Europe and the War," and a "positive Europeanism" based on love was to become the basis of the journal's platform. Under Schickele, *Die weissen Blätter* turned against the nationalism of the German press and of writers like Gerhart Hauptmann and Dehmel who stirred up hatred between nations with their patriotic jingoism and Pan-Germanic mysticism, but it could be equally scathing about the biased chauvinism of anti-German writers like Anatole France. The aim of the journal, as Schickele saw it, was to bring about a readiness for understanding and reconciliation, regardless of fronts and frontiers. In this sense, Schickele stood for an "Imperialism of the Spirit" and defined *Die weissen Blätter* as the journal of those young Germans who even in this war wanted to remain Europeans. Schickele's Alsatian background is generally singled out as the personal reason for this attitude, and it is true that he felt equally attached to both France and Germany and, hence, was deeply divided in his loyalties because of the war, a tragic division to which he gave expression in his play *Hans im Schnakenloch* (Jack of Midge Hole), written in 1914.

*Jack of Midge Hole* is clearly an Expressionist play, though without the excesses of language and form committed by some of Schickele's contemporaries.[2] The Schnakenloch (Midge Hole) is an estate near Strasbourg. Its owner, Hans Boulanger, is a likeable rogue with a big heart and a passionate, pleasure-seeking nature, who has brought the estate to the brink of ruin by grandiose schemes which he has not had the tenacity to see through to a successful conclusion. His brother Balthasar is almost his exact opposite. He is hard-working, upright, reliable, with a highly developed sense of duty, but otherwise rather dull. The contrast between the two indicates differences between French and German national characteristics rather than between two individuals. The same kind of distinction is marked between Hans' wife, the German girl Klär, and his French mistress, Louise. Just as Hans is drawn alternately to the one woman or the other, so he is drawn toward France or Germany. Louise exercises quasi-magic powers over him and is capable of attracting him almost subconsciously against his will; Klär, on the other hand, has nothing of the enchantress about her. She is faithful and true to Hans alone and almost awe-inspiring in the purity of her love. This conflict might have resolved itself, for Hans is prepared to mend his ways and become more regular in his habits, but the war intervenes, bringing all the latent individual, racial, and cultural antagonisms to a head. Hans (and the suffering he goes through before making his decision) is the symbolic heart of the play: he stands for all men pulled by powerful forces in different directions. In the end, he reluctantly decides to join the French army because the Germans have the greater prospect of victory, while Balthasar, his brother, experiences the war as a liberation, almost as revenge for the way Hans has treated him.

On the whole, the message of the play is quite clear, namely the rejection of war, which is seen as "one single tear in the eye of the Lord." War means that "everything mankind held most dear is shouted down, all faith, the work of millions of lives, all love, all personal fates," and so it is clearly human values above all else that count for Schickele. He does not come down on the side of the French against the Germans: he wants to be with the weak against the strong. This is not a political play: it is a cry from the heart. Nevertheless, such works are not popular in wartime, and when it appeared in print in 1915 it was almost as bitterly criticized by the French as it was by the Germans, each side seeing it as propaganda for the other. It came as no surprise to anyone when Schickele emigrated to Switzerland in 1916, where, in the company of like-minded spirits (e.g., Hesse, Frank, Werfel, and Unruh), he developed his journal *Die weissen Blätter* into the leading organ for radical but undogmatic pacifism.

## II  *Gustav Sack*

Another work from this period which gives testimony to the agonies suffered by some intellectuals over the causes and implications of the war is the play *Refraktär* (Refractory) by Gustav Sack (1885–1916). Sack was an exponent of Expressionist narrative prose, and yet this author, who was only once in a theater in his life, who rejected Strindberg and ignored the dramatic experiments of the Expressionists, turned exceptionally to the dramatic form in 1916 to deal with the problem of the war. Should one join up when war breaks out or not? Sack's letters make it clear that his is a drama of decision, like Schickele's, and that at first he was by no means clear in his own mind how it would end. He had almost decided to make his hero join up after all, when he had him jump to his death. This was not the decision made by Sack himself who, after an initial refusal to join the colors, capitulated and served on the Western Front until 1916. *Refractory*, a clearly autobiographical work, was completed during a sick leave before Sack was moved to Romania, where he was killed in December, 1916.

Sack's play, which is fairly traditional in language and form, despite the tendency toward monologues, focuses on one central figure, Egon, in his period of decision. Karl Eibl has summarized the classical form of the play as: Protagonist-Frau-Pöbel.[3] The protagonist, Egon, is held by the woman, Mignon. His love for her is his only attachment to the social sphere. The third main character, Jakob Vogel, is a journalist and, therefore, by definition, one who professionally debases the word, an exponent of empty phrases. Mignon flirts with Jakob, who flirts with a serving girl. When news of the outbreak of hostilities arrives, Egon refuses to take any part in this war; he is "refractory." But then Jakob, too, decides to be refractory, turning Egon's individual decision into a journalistic gesture. Thereupon Egon decides to join the colors after all, only to change his mind once more in reaction to his jingoistic father-in-law. In the end, Vogel goes off to the war and Egon does not. This makes him a social outcast, even Mignon leaves him, and he destroys his manuscripts and climbs upward into a mountain wasteland, where he finds death. Sack's play is far from being a great work, but there is a representative quality about its attempt to deal, not only with the causes of the war and the pressures it places upon the individual, but also with the impossible isolation and alienation of that individual once he has turned against war. For the individual without the support of a party or a creed, nothing is left after his quest for purity but isolation and death.

H. F. Garten has singled out the year 1916 as marking the turning point in the general attitude to the war. Until then, support for the war had been widespread. But gradually "a premonition of coming disaster dawned upon the more far-sighted."[4] From 1916 on, a string of plays critical of the war was written, published, and in some cases even produced despite the strict censorship. Of these the best known are Reinhard Goering's *Naval Encounter*, Stefan Zweig's *Jeremiah*, and Fritz von Unruh's *One Family*.

Very much in the biblical strain of Carl Hauptmann's *War, a Te Deum*, Zweig's *Jeremiah* (1919) was the first clear denunciation of war in dramatic form. The rather over-elaborate, flowery rhetoric of this vast work has lost much of its power for the modern audience; nevertheless, Garten has rightly singled out the powerful antiwar protest of some passages. As in *War, a Te Deum*, the people are easily swept along by the glorious visions conjured up by the war party. This time the true leader, however, is a prophetic seer who resists the trend of popular excitement and denounces war: "War is a wild and wicked beast, he eats the flesh from the strong and sucks the marrow from the mighty ones, he crushes the cities between his jaws and with his hooves he tramples the land." The pacifist tendency is quite outspoken, and the play ends with a rhapsodic plea for "a gospel of brotherhood and redemption through suffering. Defeat ... is a blessing bestowed by God to purify the hearts of man."[5]

## III  *Fritz von Unruh*

Gustav Sack pondered over the possibilities of a refusal to fight; in the end, however, like so many others he joined the army, fought and died. Fritz von Unruh (1885–1970), on the other hand, was to be one of the few to survive the war; he lived on to become one of the leading figures of the Weimar Republic. He was even to survive internment in France in 1940 and exile in the U.S.A. during the Second World War. One could hardly have predicted that Germany's leading pacifist and republican writer was to come from a famous military family—von Unruh was the son of a general—yet even his earlier works (e.g., *Offiziere* [Officers, 1911] and *Louis Ferdinand Prinz von Preussen* [1913]) deal with themes of rebellion. Fritz von Unruh went through the same moral and intellectual turmoil as Sack before arriving at his decision, and yet how much greater the conflict between education and breeding on the one hand and self-determination and the family code on the other must have been in his case. Encouraged to write by the Army High Command, he was so shattered by what he saw of the battles for Verdun, in which 300,000 men died on the German side alone, that he composed his first outspokenly antiwar piece, *Opfergang* (Sacrifice). This work and the next, *Vor der Entscheidung* (Before the Decision), were immediately banned, and von Unruh had to appear before a war tribunal. Acquitted, he returned to the front, where in the little town of Merles he wrote *One Family* at the height of an artillery bombardment. Like *Sacrifice*, this work was branded by the Army High Command as mere hallucination; however, it was published in 1917 by Kurt Wolff and left with the Max Reinhardt-Bühnen in October 1917 for performance. Gerhart Hauptmann himself was to introduce it, but because of the ban on the work by the Army authorities it never appeared on the Reinhardt stage until after the war, in December, 1918. Remarkably enough, however, the play *was* performed elsewhere during the war despite the censorship. The première was a performance before an invited audience

in June, 1918, in the Frankfurt Schauspielhaus under the direction
of Heinz Herald. The impact on the audience, aware of the
failure of the German offensives on the Western Front and
longing for peace, was enormous; following this performance the
book quickly sold 25,000 copies. Shortly afterwards the war
was over.

Unruh's *One Family* is the first part of a trilogy. The second
part, *Platz* (Place), was begun in 1917, but completed and
published in 1920. The third and final part, *Dietrich*, was begun
in the 1920's, but not completed until 1945. Until the publication
of Unruh's *Gesammelte Werke* in 1972 it was impossible to
examine the three parts of the trilogy together. Only *One Family*
will be analyzed here as showing a representative Expressionist
reaction in dramatic form to the war. According to one critic,
the manuscript of *One Family* is spattered with blood and
"there is on every page a footnote, a short prayer, written because, as the poet once said, he did not know whether he would
still be alive when the page should be turned."[6] There is no
such blood-stained manuscript in the Literaturarchiv in Marbach
which now holds all of Unruh's literary remains; however, there
is no doubt that von Unruh did write his play in the very heat
of the battle. It is possible that he then pared and pruned the
original more extensive, expansive work. *One Family* is Kleistian
in tone and in language and highly classical in form, a one-acter
lasting about one hour in performance. For a war play, *One
Family* is remarkable in that war itself is not its subject. The
action is removed out of time and place, indeed from the sphere
of modern civilization and all its trappings, and deliberately
situated in a zone which encourages a mythical interpretation.
There is no identifiable plot, and every account of the play
differs from the next in fundamental details. Some clear images
do, however, emerge.

The title *One Family* seems deliberately archaic in its suggestion of an earlier, primeval form of family structure. This
clan or tribe consists of a mother (but no father), a daughter,
and three sons. The action takes place above the battle outside
a graveyard on a hillside, where the mother of this ancient race
with her daughter and youngest son is busy preparing the grave
for her favorite son, who has fallen in battle. While the three

are still digging, soldiers bring the two other sons in chains, one of them a coward who has refused to obey orders, and the oldest son who has broken the military code and defiled the honor of the army by raping a woman of the enemy side. Both are to die and are chained to the wall of the graveyard. When the youngest son fails to execute them, the soldiers depart with him for fresh combat and a family debate begins between the mother, the eldest son, and the daughter. Except for his screams, the cowardly son is silent throughout.

There develops a battle between the younger generation and the old, between the chaos which the war has unleashed and the order of an earlier world. The daughter releases the eldest son from his chains, and in the wildness of their incestuous lust they almost fling themselves on each other, regardless of the mother's presence. The old bonds of morality have broken down in the war—why should they be restricted by ancient laws? After all, if blame is to be apportioned, is it not basically the mother's fault? Is it not always the mother who is responsible for all the horrors of life? For is it not the mother who populates the world and makes children believe in antiquated concepts, fairy tales, religions, so that they have no knowledge of the world as it really is? Brother and sisters feel that they have grown up in a world of lies, which keeps them remote from life, hence their hatred for the older generation and their rejection of faith and fatherland. The violence of the play is incredible, but it is a violence in words alone, although incest and murder seem close to realization. The oldest son does actually desecrate the graves of the dead, thereby rejecting the world of the mother, who sends her favorite son to his death on the battlefield. He then closes the gates, climbs the graveyard wall, and plunges from there to his death. The daughter, hearing the victorious army returning up the mountain, flees among the graves from what is coming, uttering the dreadful words: "I destroy the organ of reproduction."

When the victorious leaders arrive, they attempt to have the body of the oldest son dragged away, but the mother and her youngest son stop them. The mother fights with the leader for his field marshal's staff of authority and wins it from him. Now the mother goes through a transformation. Where before she had stood for the ancient laws, she now takes up the ideas of the younger generation and, like her son, turns against law and order for its own sake. She speaks the words that seem to foreshadow the theme of Brecht's *Caucasian Chalk Circle*: "Es wandelt sich auch Recht!" ("The law too changes"), and the enthusiasm of her illumination carries the army along with her. The soldiers cast off their weapons and turn with her toward a new future. If mothers have been decisive in sending their sons to their deaths in battle in the past, then it is the mothers who must point the new direction for the future. Accordingly, she casts the symbolic staff of leadership from her. But such rebellion is dangerous, for it touches religion and disturbs the state; and for this she must die, as she does, uttering the Kleistian words, with their echoes of Penthesilea's suicide:

Hier, hier und da, stosst alle Eisenschäfte mir tief ins Blut! Ich will sie so zerschmelzen, dass meinen Kindern keine Schmerzen bleiben!

(Here, here and there too, plunge all your steel shafts into my blood! I'll melt them down till nothing remains to harm by children.)

She is pushed onto the burial mounds, whereupon the daughter bites herself free of the soldiers' grasp and creeps away into the undergrowth. But what the mother now represents by her transformation can no longer be denied, and the men raise the youngest son onto their shoulders before rushing back to the valley toward a new life and a new age.

If *One Family* is somewhat difficult to understand because of the abstract nature of its language, the general significance of the play nevertheless emerges fairly clearly. This is yet another Expressionist drama of decision; indeed, as Judith A. Taylor has put it: "the entire family stands at a point of existential decision between life and death."[7] As the play closes, the daughter and the cowardly son have not yet made their decision; their fate is not revealed until the sequel *Platz*. The youngest son does opt for life and sets out to reform society, but here, too, it is left to the sequel to show how he fares. So the real action of *One Family* is concentrated on the discussion between the mother and the eldest son. In an extremely Expressionistic manner, the eldest son demands absolute freedom, and in Nietzschean, Dionysian language presses his demands even beyond the normal taboos of *Geschlecht* (which means sex as well as family). He desires his sister, threatens to kill his mother, and denounces his father. The aim of his Expressionistic quest is to penetrate through all myths to the truth:

The life cycle seems to the eldest son meaningless and he is bent upon discovering meaning. His desire to lift the veil, to penetrate the darkness is the typical Expressionist search for the essential, the *Sein*, like the Bettler's wish to tear away the curtain of *Schauspielerei*. Unruh's Ältester compares himself to light, he speaks repeatedly of his *Geist*, which refuses to become fogged by the riddles of the mother.[8]

As far as the mother is concerned, the death of this son represents the Expressionist theme of the awakening or transformation. His death is part of the progression toward the New Man, and her awakening comes when she realizes her duty to proclaim the birth of the New Man. So she dies, but her dream of the new life will be accomplished after her death by her youngest son.

If the strengths of the play were immediately apparent to a wartime audience experiencing its onslaught with the end of hostilities already in sight, it must be admitted that they have faded with time. Unruh's work has not worn well, and his struggle for abstraction and elevated style has resulted in an excessive ballast of metaphor and imagery. Even at the time the famous critic Julius Bab claimed that after four or five readings he had still failed to grasp its intent, and *he* was a practiced reader of dramatic texts. The unpracticed reader is liable to fare even worse.[9] Pathos was the favored mode of the Expressionists, but here it is taken too far. The same applies both to plot and to characterization. No trace whatsoever is left of the reality of the Great War, and the characters likewise have become reduced, not expanded, to symbols demonstrating and permutating certain existential situations.

## IV  *Reinhard Goering*

Closer to the realities of modern warfare, though still very classical in format, is a play by Reinhard Goering (1887–1936)

about a battle at sea. May 31, 1916, has gone down in history
as the date of the battle of the Skagerrak. On that day, the
German fleet met the English Grand Fleet in the only grand-
scale naval encounter of the war. In this battle, the greatest
in world history, no clear-cut victory had been won by nightfall,
but English losses in men and ships were severe, and hence
Skagerrak was acclaimed in Germany as a decisive turning point,
even though the German fleet was to take no further part in
the course of the war. Skagerrak became a name to conjure
with, a name like Tannenberg and Langemarck, symbolizing
for Germans the epitome of heroism.

By choosing a battleship as the setting for his play, Goering
proved extremely prescient, for the battleship as the microcosm of life and death in a wartime situation was soon to
become a literary fashion, resulting in plays like Theodor
Plievier's *Der Kaisers Kulis* (The Emperor's Coolies), Ernst
Toller's *Feuer aus den Kesseln* (Draw the Fires), and Friedrich
Wolf's *Die Matrosen von Cattaro* (The Sailors of Cattaro). The
most famous work of this kind was not a play, but a film,
Sergei Eisenstein's *Battleship Potemkin*, which had a profound
effect throughout the world. Yet even in listing these works a
paradox becomes apparent. *Battleship Potemkin* is based on
the revolt by Russian sailors in November, 1917, and marks
the beginning of the Russian Revolution; Wolf's play is based
on an abortive revolt by sailors of the Austro-Hungarian fleet
at Cattaro in the Adriatic; the German Revolution of 1918 was
started by sailors based in Kiel. Accordingly, battleships and
sailors are associated in the German mind with revolution, while
Skagerrak is associated with victory. The question, therefore,
is whether Goering's play is patriotic or revolutionary. To this
there is no unequivocal reply; indeed, the most recent interpretation discusses it in terms of its "well-balanced polyvalence."
This goes some way toward explaining why such a play could
be performed at all in wartime, after the German sailors
Reichpietsch and Köbes had been shot for mutiny and hundreds
of others had received heavy sentences. The play *could* be seen
as a revolutionary pacifistic work, redolent with doubts about
the meaningfulness of the conflict, filled with longings for peace;
but at the same time, in its apparent acceptance of the fateful-

ness of events and in the resignation of its ending, it was
certainly far from being a directly defeatist work and therefore
presented no direct challenge to the authorities.

Otto F. Best has classified the three fundamental possibilities
of reaction in the face of death depicted by Goering in this
play as follows: (1) Devout Christian acceptance of fate; (2)
Buddhist attitude of suffering without emotion; (3) intellectual
rebellion, resulting in a "Wandlung," a transformation in the
direction of a new man capable of realizing the full potential
of Man and of life.[10] There is plenty of evidence of all three
of these basic attitudes distributed over the arguments and
discussions between the sailors, but never in a way liable to
alter events in the real world. Instead, Goering has deliberately
removed the action to an almost classical Greek setting marked
by choral elements and Socratic dialogue. The first full production in Berlin went even further. Reinhardt himself did
the *mise-en-scène*, and the casting for the sailors included some
of the most famous names in German theater history: Hermann
Thimig, Conrad Veidt, Emil Jannings, Paul Wegener, and Werner
Krauss.

Heinz Herald, who was responsible for the whole Junges
Deutschland series, has given his Expressionistic view of the play:

Strange, that nobody ever got round to saying it: this is no gun-
turret, this is a human body. And the individual voices are voices
within a Man's breast—a strict man, the dreamer, the man who has
premonitions, the rough, lusty man and the revolutionary mutineer,
anarchist: that is what a Man looks like inside, these are all voices
speaking against each other, with each other, inside of us.[11]

Nothing could be further from the reality of Skagerrak, and
yet, unlike Fritz von Unruh's *One Family*, the play does have
the feel of modern warfare. War is a devouring monster, a
beast, but it can also be a machine, a mighty Juggernaut which,
once on the move, rolls on irrevocably over puny mankind—
such is the feeling imparted by Reinhard Goering's play, *Naval
Encounter* (1916/17).

The drama is also decidedly Expressionistic in form and
content. War is no longer fought around romantic Napoleonic

bivouacs by a colorful *soldateska*: it has become the mechanical warfare of the modern age. Not that war is presented with any realistic detail—on the contrary, the stylization is now complete, the compression to abstract form extreme, the process of depersonalization total. The bare gun turret and the menacing efficiency of the naval gun dominate the scene, while the sailors serving it are reduced to mere numbers. In some productions, the gun was not even there—the puppet-like slaves went through the balletic motions of aiming and firing a nonexistent gun, while the action toward the end was punctuated by flashes, bangs, and screams.

Goering's drama is a typically Expressionistic scream play (*Schreidrama*). It begins with a shout, and there are plenty of screams and shouts before the end. But the most striking feature of the play is the tight discipline and the controlled, hard, highly stylized language employed to express the feverish atmosphere. This is a marked development from the Neo-Romantic diction of Carl Hauptmann and the excessively flowery periods of Werfel's *Jeremiah*. Yet the prose is still poetic in the new Expressionist manner and can easily be printed in lines like verse. The quick switches from short, sharp stichomythic utterances of classical brevity to long monologues of considerable eloquence is a feature of the Expressionist style which revels in the conjunction of extremes—ice-cold with fever-heat, compression with expansiveness, logicality with ecstasy, static with dynamic.

Characteristically, too, there is little or no plot—merely the suffocating situation of seven men moving toward apparently inevitable death. The talk is of signs at sea, girls, the enemy, and death. Sleep alternates with wakefulness, dream with reality. The climax of the play is the discussion between the First Sailor and the Fifth Sailor on the problem of obedience and mutiny. Significantly, the First Sailor is the religious seeker who keeps looking for a sign and longs to know what the Higher Powers want of us, while the Fifth is the man who can no longer follow the instinctive behavior patterns of his parents, the rationalist whose brain is surrounded by a buzzing swarm which threatens to suck it dry. He denies all knowledge of the Higher Powers.

Totally Expressionistic is the Socratic dialogue which develops between these two men, where by a question-and-answer game an attempt is made to arrive at truth. In the modern German context, the question becomes particularly significant when the Fifth Gunner asks: "Can madness not reign over a whole nation and sway even its leader? Must we do the will of madmen?" What is the purpose of life on earth? To serve God, as the First Gunner claims? To this problem the Fifth gives the typical Expressionist answer: "Not having Him do you have all, but having self you have all." Here the untranslatable German *Mensch* is the key word, namely self, individual human being, mortal Man. The Socratic dialogue has now reached a point where war can be clearly denounced as madness and as a crime against mankind: "there is a certain bond between man and man: obeying it is a more sacred duty than anything else worth fighting for." With this conviction of the individual's duty toward his fellow men, the Fifth Sailor can now express his determination to refuse to fight; he will mutiny even against "the merciless force, against something all are subject to and everyone bows down to . . . something no-one can revolt against." It is, therefore, always possible for the individual to assert himself and refuse to fight, no matter how overwhelming the forces against him may be. At this point, however, the others awaken and overhear and immediately it is demonstrated that mutinous talk and intellectual discussion are not the deciding factors, for even the firmest resolve cannot stand firm against the *Rausch* of action when enemy ships are sighted.

Whereas up to this point the play has been static, relying on the verbal exchanges of the seven sailors, all now becomes dynamic as they prepare for battle. They are swept along by the feverish intoxication of battle, including the Fifth Sailor. It is the test of battle which the Fourth Sailor says will show the New Man whom this age has produced. Action may mean death, but for a brief moment one is living at fullest capacity. The Fifth Sailor now says: "I like action. It will cost us our lives any minute. But till then our lungs heave, hearts race, muscles jump. All that damned questioning, lads, where's it gone?" This is exactly the abandonment of reason portrayed in Carl Hauptmann's play, exactly the same escape from the curse of excessive cerebration into hyperemia, the *Rausch* which led

Gottfried Benn to accept, at least for a time, the Nazi mythology.

By the end of the play, the gunners are gas-masked and indistinguishably fused into an anonymous fighting body. All individuality has been sacrificed to the group united in common action, and all are soon dead or dying, with the exception of the Fifth Sailor who is left to answer the question: why did he not mutiny after all? He could have mutinied, and it might have had some effect; but it is so much easier just to fire a gun, to submerge individuality in group allegiance, so much more difficult to stand up against one's fellows and the whole trend of the time. So the idea of mutiny raised in the play is lost again. Men are still no more than tiny cogs in a mighty war machine over which they have no control. Can they even be held responsible for their actions?

> Seht! Seht!
> Der Weg ist nicht gewählt von uns,
> die Hände nicht geführt von uns.
> Doch, doch wir taten es,
> wir führten unsere Hände.
> Uns ist die Schuld.

> (See, see we did not choose the way, we
> had no power over the hands we raised.
> Yes, yes, we did do it, did act, did
> raise our hands. Ours is the guilt.)

The whole work has the style and rigor of a classical tragedy with its constant suggestion of forces outside man (Higher Powers) controlling his destiny. Yet the final outcome is not fatalism but the idea that the individual must stand out against the forces that threaten to control him; he must act for the good of humanity. Man's duty to man is the final arbiter.

## V  *Walter Hasenclever*

Ulrich Weisstein has described Goering's *Naval Encounter* as an *Antigone* in disguise: "The thematic parallels between *Seeschlacht* and *Antigone* extend even beyond the Antigone-Ismene conflict, although they are nowhere as visible as in the

ideological struggle between sailors one and five."[12] An un-
disguised Expressionist *Antigone* was to appear from the pen
of Walter Hasenclever. In 1916 Hasenclever was on the Eastern
Front and in Dresden. This was where his *Antigone* was written,
to be performed, astonishingly, in December 1917, in the
Schauspielhaus of the Leipzig Stadttheater.[13] That a performance
of the play should have been permitted says something for the
advantages of a "timeless" classical guise, but the significance
of the Antigone theme in wartime should have been clear enough.
In any event, the impact was enormous. There was a veritable
tidal wave of reviews and commentaries, and in the same year
Hasenclever was awarded the Kleist Prize, joining von Unruh,
Sorge, and Barlach as winners of this honor.

Hölderlin's *Antigone* was a favorite of the Expressionist generation, but Hasenclever, in fact, goes back beyond it to the
Sophoclean drama. For the first three acts at least he follows
Sophocles closely; but though the guise is ancient, the action
and the actors have been transposed into the modern world.
Creon is now the last representative of a doomed monarchy;
the chorus, which, in the Greek original, is very much in the
background, now assumes almost a leading role as People of
Thebes, and by placing the Volk at the head of his *dramatis
personae*, Hasenclever shows that he means the masses, doomed
to much suffering and confusion, but always ready for the
revelation, to take a larger part in the action: Antigone has
been removed from the sphere of cult and myth and is now
the proclaimer of Christian love and humanity, the savior of an
enslaved people. Hasenclever had no doubt whatsoever about
the intention underlying his play:

My version of the *Antigone* of Sophocles has a political aim. Written
in 1916 at a time when every free word was subject to censorship,
it had the task of protesting in ancient guise against war and
rape. So I saw in Antigone a figure of love and humanity, who
buries the enemy, her brother, although the king has expressly for-
bidden it. The individual fate was raised to the universal, the old
myth received a new import. The tragedy became a war cry against
the power principle embodied in Kreon and his regime. Antigone's
sacrificial death meant the victory of the idea and at the same time
the release of a defenseless misguided people.[14]

Hasenclever's *Antigone* is far more violent and outspoken than Goering's carefully balanced work. Hasenclever was already famous for *The Son* (1914). *The Son* is clearly a work of protest with all the merits and demerits of Angry Young Man violence; even if its long and turbulent emotional monologues were all severely pruned, the melodramatic excesses of the play could have little appeal to the present-day audience. With *Antigone*, however, Hasenclever moved from the middle-class milieu of his drama of social protest back to classical antiquity for his denunciation of war. According to Garten, his *Antigone* "presents a perfect example of the Expressionist style: the language, austere and sparing, is shorn of all poetic adornments and occasionally rises to impassioned outbursts always with the sole intention of conveying the author's message."[15]

In effect, the play, like Goering's *Naval Encounter*, is characterized by the combination of extremes—classical brevity alternating with long monologues, static with dynamic features, logicality with ecstasy. Now, however, instead of the stifling atmosphere of a naval gun turret in a modern battleship, Hasenclever, who was writing the play while with the German Army on the Eastern Front, constructed a play of vast scope and dimensions. Remembering a spectacular Reinhardt production of Sophocles' *Oedipus Rex* in a great hall, he wrote his *Antigone* for an amphitheater. The stage is split into two levels, a raised platform is the theater of the king, while an arena is the theater of the people. Spotlights pick out one area or the other, as required.

The message of the play is the gospel of love and human brotherhood combined with a denunciation of war. Creon, the cruel king and tyrant, is given words of Emperor William II to speak, so that the contemporary reference is unmistakable despite the classical setting. A striking feature of this play, as indeed of all Expressionist plays from Hauptmann's *War, a Te Deum* on, is that the People are presented as a more or less mindless mass, to be moved in one direction or the other by the arguments of the opposing factions. In fact, despite the vast scope and the *Sturm und Drang* violence with which the Antigone theme is treated, the play resolves itself into the typical Expressionist confrontation between two dominant personalities representative of dialectically opposed points of view, in this case Creon and Antigone. The people are swayed in one direction or the other. The play, in effect, progresses in a sequence of speech and counter-speech, argument and counter-argument, until by the force of the dialectic, even the tyrant Creon himself, who has lived by the dead letter of the law, is made to see the error of his ways and hand over power to the people.

Antigone's eyes have been opened by the blind Oedipus, who has shown her the nature of true human goodness and love; and this, in turn, is the gospel she preaches to the masses. She conjures up apocalyptic images of the doom and destruction that ensue when mankind goes mad in war, and warns the people against the easy temptation to revel in military glory. While the horrors of war conjured up by Antigone's words are powerful enough, the second act sees the arrival of a true visionary, the prophet Teiresias, who is capable of creating a living image of war before the tyrant's eyes:

*Heaps of dead. People with gaping wounds. Women, men with daggers in their chests. Demented bleating like animals. Smashed limbs. Children stumble among the bodies.*                Act III, sc. vi[16]

Equally typical of the Expressionist drama is the exemplary suicide of Antigone—a strange manner (it might be thought) of leading the way toward a regeneration of mankind, but the one taken by Eustache de Saint Pierre in Kaiser's *Burghers of Calais*, Grete in Toller's *Hinkemann*, and many other Expressionist visionaries. Antigone leads the way and is followed by Haemon, the king's son, who abandons the cult of the sword and kills himself beside her body after calmly stabbing at his tyrant father Creon. So "the first man of the new earth is converted by her grave." Just as characteristic of the Expressionist drama is the destruction of the city by fire with which the fourth act concludes.

As has been seen, the Expressionist generation was obsessed by the need for the eradication of the old way of life and constantly conjured up such images of the twilight of mankind. A new dawn is about to break, the rich and the mighty have fallen, and the day of the people is at hand:

Paläste wanken. Die Macht ist zu Ende.
Wer gross war, stürzt in den Abgrund,
Die Tore donnern zu.
Wer alles besass, hat alles verloren;
Folgt mir! Ich will euch führen.
Der Wind steigt aus den Trümmern,
Die neue Welt bricht an.

(Palaces totter. Might has had its day.
He who was great, plunges to his doom,
The gates thunder shut.
He who possessed all, has lost all. . . .
Follow me! I will lead you.
The wind rises from the ruins.
The new world dawns.)

Act V, sc. ii[17]

Creon voluntarily relinquishes power, his spirit broken by the deaths of Antigone, Haemon, and his queen Eurydice. The new leader to emerge is a simple man of the people. Anarchy threatens, but a voice from the tomb reminds mankind of the example of Antigone and all fall on their knees.

Clearly, such a play is politically naive and melodramatically exaggerated in its piling up of horrors, warriors on horseback charging across the arena, visions of war, multiple deaths, and extraordinary conversions. Nevertheless, the exuberant theatricality of the play is never in doubt and strikingly reinforces the outspoken indictment of war.

CHAPTER 5

# Revolution: Rubiner, Toller, Jung, Becher, Wolf

## I  Expressionism and Politics

HOW political was Expressionism in general and Expressionist drama in particular? It is easy to dismiss the Expressionists as vague enthusiasts ("Schwärmer") with little or no feeling for the realities of politics; and indeed this has often been done, for example, by Robert Musil, who said:

What Expressionism likes, above all else, is a sort of barking at ideas, for, in effect, is the appeal to grand ideas of humanity like Suffering, Love, Eternity, Goodness, Lust, Prostitution, Blood, Chaos, with the help of double exclamation marks instead of question marks, any more valuable than the lyrical activity of a dog barking at the moon . . . ?[1]

Siegfried Melchinger, who raises the general question of revolution in his book *Geschichte des politischen Theaters* (1971), is tempted to dismiss most Expressionist dramatists as unworthy of notice in his general survey but singles out Sternheim and Kaiser as the truly revolutionary forces in the drama of the time. Indeed, any consideration of the plays of Sternheim and Kaiser in the period of World War I shows that they were far from vague or confused in their social and political vision of the world. On the contrary, they were quite specific in their views about where the world was going. This same political-ethical concern, in fact, characterizes the whole Expressionist generation, though it was no more successful in formulating solutions to the problems of the age than the professional politicians. Gruber has pointed out that a journal like *Die Aktion* "combined radicalism in politics and aesthetics from its beginning in 1911. Heinrich Mann, who became the intellectual ancestor and advisor of later Expressionism, laid the political cornerstone of the movement in his essay of 1910 titled *Geist und Tat*. Here he directed German writers to become agitators and to ally themselves with the people against authority."[2]

As Gruber develops his argument on the political-ethical mission of German Expressionism and the Expressionists' belief in the integral relationships between literature and politics, it becomes clear that they did believe literature capable of changing the world. They—the writers and dramatists—were the leaders, especially since the traditional leaders had failed. Not surprisingly, therefore, they tended in their plays to look for a spiritual rather than a political revolution. Man would become the measure of all things, but the soul and spirit of man had been distorted and buried by the world; hence, the new world would be brought about when man rediscovered himself:

Although they held society responsible for man's spiritual perversion, the Expressionists decided that it was more important to restore man from within than to alter society's effect on him, or at least they believed that the alteration of society depended upon the transformation of man. The conviction became widespread that the discoveries, or laws, or inventions of the world could not save man: that only he could save himself. But how?[3]

Generally speaking, politics was not the way, and this is not surprising in a country where politics as represented by parties and factions had until then abysmally failed. Germany had always looked for a strong man like Frederick the Great or Bismarck; and this was the way the Expressionists chose as well—only now the great leader would be a Nietzschean superman and spiritual leader toward Utopia, rather than a politician.

When the Revolution broke out in November, 1918, the Expressionists were immediately as involved in it as they were in the war itself; and, indeed, the problems it presented were, to a large extent, the same. To what extent was one justified in using force and violence to change society? How much could the individual achieve on his own, and to what extent was he committed to collective action? Just as there was no doubt about the overall pacifist direction of the Expressionist movement, so too there was no doubt about the pro-revolutionary sympathies of most Expressionists. In general, their sympathy was with socialism and political parties of the left, and only very few (like Arnolt Bronnen and Hanns Johst) moved to the right. As far as the political parties were concerned, the SPD had tarnished its image for most intellectuals by its support for the war credits; and, besides, it tended to appear as an anti-intellectual, bureaucratic, heartless party machine. Hence, the affiliation of most intellectuals was with the Independent Socialist Party; so much so, indeed, that George Lukács has tried to characterize the political stance of Expressionism by almost exclusive reference to the USPD. Some were to move further left to join the Spartacists, but only Becher was to become a full-time and life-long member of the Communist Party (KPD). It is for this reason that Expressionism for long languished in the German Democratic Republic after the Second World War under the blanket dismissal of having failed to foresee the true course of history and ally itself with the cause of the victorious proletariat. Hiller's *Logokratie* or rule by an intellectual élite and the creation of a *Politischer Rat Geistiger Arbeiter*, which found the most widespread support among Expressionist intellectuals, is the most conspicuous example of complete divorce between the ideal and reality which is so characteristic of this kind of "political" thinking.

Its program was a combination of activist pacifism, political action, economic reform and utopianism. It proposed the formation of a league of nations and world parliament, the universal abolition of conscription and the prohibition of all military arrangements, the punishment by economic sanction of all disturbers of the peace, the just distribution of material possessions, the confiscation of "excess" property, and the abolition of capital punishment.[4]

This program was enough to terrify the bourgeoisie and confirm its fears about the revolutionary nature of Expressionism, but no one needed to have any worries, for there was no machinery for putting any of these proposals into practice.

## II  *Ludwig Rubiner*

Very close to the activist Hiller was Ludwig Rubiner (1881–1920), author of one play, *Die Gewaltlosen* (Those without Violence), which he wrote in Zurich in 1917/18. As Rubiner himself described the genesis of his work, "The writing of this legend was begun in January, 1917, completed in the autumn of 1918. In the midst of the hardest years of desperation, while the victories of world capitalism trundled backwards and forwards over nations."[5] Characteristically, very little is known about Rubiner's personal life, because he thought the individual unimportant and the collective spirit of the community everything:

Ludwig Rubiner desires no biography of himself. He believes that not only the recording of happenings but also the recording of works and dates derive from a pretentious and antiquated image of the individualistic, dressing-gowned artist. He is of the conviction that what is important for the present and the future is anonymous, creative adherence to the community.[6]

However, a little *is* known about Rubiner's early life and works. Around 1910 he came to Berlin and became very closely associated with Franz Pfemfert, who published his political essays in *Die Aktion*. Pfemfert, like Rubiner, was convinced that Wilhelminian Germany was heading for war, and he encouraged Rubiner to express his opposition to the militaristic mentality of the age. From 1912 onward, the aim of all of Rubiner's writing was to change the world by changing the way people think; and his essays made a powerful impact on the Expressionist generation. In 1916 his collection of essays, *Der Mensch in der Mitte* (Man in the Middle), appeared; in 1918, the almanac, *Gemeinschaft*; and in 1919 the anthology, *Kameraden der Menscheit* (Comrades of Mankind), followed. As early as 1912, Rubiner, the pacifist and socialist, had tried to define the political role of the writer:

Politics is the publication of our moral intentions. . . . I know that there is only one moral goal in life: intensity. . . . The poet participates in politics, that means he rips open, he exposes. Let him

believe in his intensity, in his explosive powers. . . . The political
poet should not exhaust his situation in insights, he ought to remove
inhibitions. In Germany, in this land of damnation and of tortures
it is not a matter of proceeding from our legend to arrive at some
truth or other. The important thing merely is that we *step out*.
The important thing now is movement, intensity and the will to
catastrophe.[7]


What Rubiner hoped to achieve was revolution without violence, brought about by changing people's consciousness and
awareness; what he did achieve was to encourage the German
contempt for politics as the art of the possible. His essays, while
claiming to be rational in their analysis of the Geist (spirit or
intellect), are turgid and obscure in the extreme and arrive at
a form of Neo-Romantic, ecstatic mysticism. His play, *Those
without Violence*, reads like an essay in semi-dramatic form,
which is how Brecht, for example, saw it: "The content of
Rubiner's play *Those without Violence*, for instance, could have
been expressed more lucidly, more attractively and in more
easily readable form in an essay. This is only an essay ruined
by being dramatized."[8]

It must be admitted that there is more than a little truth in
Brecht's comment, and yet the play exercises a strange fascination
as an absolutely consistent attempt to express a totally pacifist
position. Moreover, despite his rejection of the play, it does
anticipate Brecht in several respects—for example, in the complete disregard for the "culinary" entertainment aspects of
theater in view of the importance of the ideas to be expressed.
Hence, there is no attempt to create real-life characters; instead, "the people are representatives of ideas. A work of ideas
helps an age to arrive at its goal by going beyond time and
setting up the ultimate goal as a reality."[9]

As a presentation of the future reality of man, the work is
at the same time a pacifist protest against the present which,
despite the utterly abstract nature of the play, is clearly discernible. The background to the action is some kind of civil
war. The economic situation is desperate: innocent people are
being pursued by the police and the army; prisoners are being
abused and ill-treated; and there is more than a suggestion of

class conflict. But, in fact, it is even more difficult than is usual with Expressionist plays to extract anything identifiable as a plot, although Rubiner claimed that the modern reader could read this text as he would any gripping story.

At the beginning, at least, there is a single protagonist, a prophetic hero who proclaims a new Jerusalem. By the power of his words he is able to persuade people that pacifism is the only true path, and he gathers a nucleus of believers prepared to take the path to the new realm of freedom, love, and community spirit. The prison governor and his brutal guards are among the first converts, and on the ship the governor demonstrates his mastery of the message of nonviolence by harnessing the power of the corporate will to divert a warship that stands in their path. The will of the community has even the power to perform a miraculous cure. The possibility of a "miracle" is consistently invoked, which is perhaps not surprising in a Legende (a term that has a religious significance in Germany). This religious quality is reinforced by the Messianic charisma of the leaders and the religious ring of their language. There is no single leader in the play. The oppressed of the old society convert their oppressors and tormentors, and then they, as a collective body, take to sea. The abandoning of all force is their creed: as they see it, this is the only way of true freedom. They come to the beleaguered city, where revolutionaries are surrounded by the propertied classes (Bürger) and the starving. Here, too, they bring the message of the renunciation of force. But in the end a traitor incites the starving masses against the exponents of nonviolence whose three spokesmen, somewhat after the manner of the Burghers of Calais, make the supreme sacrifice and lay down their lives for the cause, knowing that this last act of violence against them will usher in the new realm of community, peace, and love for mankind.

What is so staggering about Rubiner's play is its intensity, its complete disregard for the rules of probability and possibility, and its single-mindedness. Rubiner had little or no knowledge of the theater, although a recent critic has seen parallels between the Neo-Romantic pageants of Eduard Stucken, which Rubiner knew, and the structure which he adopts.[10] Rubiner does not make things easy for his reader, for each page is a solid block of print with no rest for the eye. Just before his death Rubiner helped to found the Proletarian Theater in Berlin (1919), but he did not see his own play performed. The première was at the Neues Volkstheater Berlin on May 22, 1920, in the form of a memorial service for him. The production by Heinz Goldberg found favor neither with left-wing nor with right-wing critics, which was not surprising considering the extreme Expressionistic style which was essayed.[11]

The play already suffered from epic breadth, lyric pathos, and rhetoric. The visual impact must have been depressing as characters could hardly be told apart, because Goldberg dressed men, women and children all alike in grey sacking, while the meagerness of the plot was matched by the meagerness of his stage setting, which consisted of scraps of canvas and wooden poles. Green and yellow spotlights picked out the various groups from the total darkness of the stage, showing faces painted in eccentric and bright colors, and the audience was bombarded by endless screams and impassioned appeals. The result was an artistic disaster.

Rubiner's *Those without Violence* ends with a miracle, the coming to pass of the brotherhood of man. The walls of the besieged city are leveled, the trenches are filled in, and those fighting on both sides fall into each others' arms with cries of "freedom" and "brotherhood." All military ranks are abolished and the message of peace is telegraphed throughout the world. The new generation of men then sets out on the path toward eternity and new creation. The end of the war means a rebirth, the rebirth of the world. All forms of distortion and decay disappear in the new utopia. One age comes to an end, another is about to begin. All this is presented without a trace of the realities of modern warfare, or indeed of the realities of modern life as lived in the big city, and can therefore only create the impression of a bizarre form of wish fulfillment, particularly in view of the real course of events in postwar Germany, which was rent by fierce political fighting. Rubiner's play remains a failure of artistic creativity in the face of war and revolution. His pacifist creed was soon, however, to produce a sensational success in Ernst Toller's *Transfiguration*, a play which "was first written in the third year of the World Slaughter," the

final version being completed in military prison in February
and March of 1918.

### III   *Ernst Toller*

Ernst Toller (1893–1939) arrived at his revolutionary creed
by much the same path as many of his contemporaries. Surprised
in France by the outbreak of war in 1914, he immediately
made his way back to Germany to enlist, concealing a medical
condition that would have ensured him exemption in order to
do so. First with the artillery and then with the infantry he
served as a volunteer until invalided, in 1916, because of a
nervous condition. Toller's own enthusiasm and the way it
collapsed in the face of the human slaughter at the front is
the subject of his play, *Transfiguration* (1919). This play is
autobiographical in the Expressionistic manner: the path taken
by his protagonist Friedrich is Toller's own, but equally in the
Expressionistic manner, the individual experience is expanded
to embrace totality, and Friedrich becomes a figure representative for his whole generation.

But how revolutionary is Toller's play? Certainly there is no
doubt about the condemnation of militarism and all it stands
for. The grotesque scene at the beginning of the play is far
more powerful than any realistic analysis of the military caste
system could ever be. As a representative figure Friedrich has
also, without doubt, moved a long way from the jingoistic figure
at the beginning to the one who is showing sympathy with the
workers and the oppressed by the end. However, there is also
no doubt that the Strindbergian, allegorical, Christian passion
play model adopted by Toller is far more ethical-religious than
socialist-revolutionary in its impact. This did the play no harm
at the time, when it was felt to be unusually daring and dangerous, but it does make it sound comparatively harmless and
rhetorical today. It is unlikely to make any militarist or capitalist
feel uncomfortable or unsafe.

Without any doubt the most powerful parts of the play are
those that are scenic and visionary rather than rhetorical and
ethical. What Toller shows scenically can be powerful enough
to shake the most seasoned theatergoer. Perhaps the best ex-

ample of this is the light and projection effect employed in Scene vi for the hospital sequence. Seven naked war-wounded soldiers march in front of a square white canvas screen, like machines which have been specially wound up. Blinding electric light is turned on them, so that all their artificial limbs can be seen. Their bodies consist of stunted rumps without arms or legs—*all* their limbs and parts are artificial—and it is little wonder that the Friedrich figure collapses. Certainly Toller's play marked a considerable advance over Hasenclever's *The Son*, which in other respects it closely resembled. Although it adopted the principle of the single protagonist and the single perspective, the monologue no longer predominates and the dream visions alternating with the real situations allow far greater scope and range to the possible transfigurations the central figure has to undergo.

The action of the play (according to the note at the beginning) takes place in "Europe before the dawn of the rebirth," but it extends over a considerable period, showing Friedrich before and during the war; his work as an artist; his transformation; and his final participation in the revolution. Thus it is possible to see the play in the context of the 1914–18 war and after. Yet at the same time its action is abstracted from it—it is, for example, a colonial war that Friedrich fights in. Altogether the play was incredibly successful and was frequently performed. Herbert Ihering was able to describe the première by Karl Martin on October 2, 1919, as one of the "purest" theatrical evenings for a long time. In this production Expressionism was felt to be no longer mere experimentation, but to have come of age. The stage set by Robert Neppach, using suggestion instead of solid sets, reinforced the emotive quality of the text. And, of course, the acting of Fritz Kortner was sensational.[12]

What makes the work of Ernst Toller remarkable is the extent to which he lived, often with an unbearable immediacy, some of the most representative experiences of our time and in so doing obtained an unusual awareness of certain of its central tensions: tensions so insupportable that, honest as he was, he could not face all their implications, and in the end they broke him. Toller's work, at its best, represents an embodiment and exploration of these tensions:

whatever its imperfections, there is still in it an undoubted sense of a living voice with the right to speak urgently about our common condition.[13]

This is how Maurice Pittock introduces *Masse-Mensch* (Masses and Man [1920]) and the tragedy of revolution. His references to "imperfections" indicate that he is clearly aware of the weaknesses of Toller's drama, but there is equally no doubt about his recognition of the strengths of this play. Once again, as in *Transfiguration* (by general acceptance a far better play), Toller employs the device of alternating *reale Bilder* and *Traumbilder*, though the distinction between the two is not so clearly marked. Commenting later on the form of the play Toller himself expressed some doubts. As a totality, he claimed, it simply burst from him in two and a half days of feverish writing, of which the nights were haunted by grotesque demonic visions; then he had to take one year over the reworking and rewriting.

In its final form there are unreal elements in the real parts and real elements in the unreal. The whole play is in verse, though there are stylistic differences between that used in the real and the unreal sequences. Some of the speeches by the workers are also arranged in choral form, foreshadowing the direction to be taken by the proletarian drama of the 1920's and 1930's toward propagandistic *Sprechchöre*. As in *Transfiguration*, the play is clearly personal and confessional, but Toller has masked this in part by making the protagonist a woman. The dialectical nature of the work is, however, already indicated by the title *Masses and Man*, showing that, apart from the impact of chaotic events on the sensitive soul of the individual, the essence of the play will be the "duality between man as an individual and man as a social being." The play thereby becomes poetic *Seelendrama* on the one hand and an argument for or against violent revolution on the other.

In essence, the play can be reduced to a dialogue between two figures, one an allegorical representative of the revolution called Der Namenlose (The Nameless One), the other, the Woman Sonia. In this dialogue, the central problem of violence is returned to over and over again, and the play's dilemma remains unsolved—as does the author's: How can lovers of humanity overcome injustice by peaceful means when their adversaries do not hesitate to employ force against them? In the "real" sections, the course of the November Revolution in Germany can be detected easily enough, although Toller has deliberately avoided historical accuracy or identifiable person- alities and events; the particular has been expanded into the general. The same applies to the "unreal" sections which, by their dreamlike visions, "express" the developments and trans- formations taking place within the soul of the protagonist as she progresses from the naive sympathizer with the cause of revolution and the proletariat at the beginning to the unsenti- mental and experienced revolutionary at the end, who is prepared to lay down her life for the cause of nonviolence. In this way, the aspirations of the protagonist are made visible to the audience, which is encouraged to sympathize with the path she is taking; and at the same time her consciousness is ex- panded, as she herself becomes aware of wider horizons and different possibilities.

At all times, Toller points away from the individual by means of a variety of dramatic devices. Sonia, for example, is given a Doppelgänger "whose face has a magical similarity with that of the woman." Sonia's husband, too, can reappear as the clerk at the stockmarket, etc. In this way the audience is invited to make connections between characters, seeing them both as private individuals with personal feelings and as agents of the system.

*Masses and Man* was an enormous success in its own time, though it tended to be denounced in left-wing quarters for its apparent betrayal of the revolution.[14] Before all others this was the play that made Expressionism known throughout the world. It was translated into many languages and widely discussed and performed in England and America. That the National Socialists at least considered Toller a revolutionary writer is beyond question. In 1933 Hitler ordered all his works to be burned. Yet it is easy to see why Toller's plays have not survived. Brecht, whose own early plays right up to Lehrstücke like *The Measures Taken* seem as obsessed with the problem of violence as Toller's, was quick to point out the weakness of such Schillerian idealism. Nevertheless, despite rhetorical and ideological weaknesses Toller did point the way to the future. Not only did he attempt to tackle major political problems; his Expressionist drama brought a new class onto the stage—the proletariat. *Masses and Man* was dedicated to the proletariat.

Of course, there had been plays before set in the proletarian milieu, but there was now a fundamental difference between the Expressionist proletarian drama and a play like Hauptmann's *Weavers* or Büchner's *Woyzeck*. In earlier dramas, the proletarian had been an unthinking person who rebelled against his fate as a result of some vague but powerful impulse. The dramatists who created such figures aimed to move the audience to compassion for his suffering. In the modern Expressionist drama, the proletarian is active and aware, rebelling against his fate, prepared to fight for a new world and a new social structure. He is activated by understanding and insight as well as emotion. Whether Expressionism produced works of lasting value or not, there is no doubt that through proletarian drama of this kind the stage became a forum for political discussion such as it had not been since the days of Schiller's *Robbers* and *Love and Intrigue*. The future of proletarian drama in Germany was to lie not so much with Toller as with men like Friedrich Wolf, Franz Jung, Johannes R. Becher and Bertolt Brecht who did throw in their lot wholeheartedly with that of the working classes.

## IV   *Franz Jung*

Franz Jung (1888–1963) has, until recently, been one of the forgotten men of the Expressionist generation, but in the increasing wave of interest in the political rather than lyrical wing of Expressionism he, too, has been rediscovered and his work exhumed and republished. His life was one of the most colorful and eventful in an eventful age, and his literary career was equally checkered. After studying law, he became a commercial journalist specializing in stock market reports. This expertise was to prove a very valuable source of income, and he was constantly to return to it when his artistic activities went amiss. Among his first dramatic works was a *Puppenspiel* (Puppet Play) published in *Der Sturm* (1912); and from 1912 on he published prose works, most notably *Das Trottelbuch* (The Blockhead Book), and was close to the *Aktion* circle around Pfemfert. Here he met Ludwig Rubiner, whose "The Poet Intervenes in Politics" made a deep impression on him, got to know the activists Karl Otten and Kurt Hiller, as well as Carl Einstein, Sternheim, and Landauer; and was associated with Landauer's anarchist-syndicalist group *Die Tat* (The Deed).

Jung was noted for his bohemian life and was known to have lived as a newsvendor and tramp (an almost pre-Brechtian predilection for the asocial existence). He protested against the war, was drafted and subsequently sent to Spandau prison for desertion. Here he wrote his novels *Sophie, Opferung* (Sacrifice), and *Der Sprung in die Welt* (The Leap into the World), which were published by Pfemfert. By way of the lunatic asylum, he was released from military service and took up stockmarket reporting again. In the last years of the war he opened an insurance office in Hamburg which became one of the centers for the scattered Spartacus groups. By 1918 he was involved with the political wing of Berlin Dada. George Grosz described him at that time as a violent Rimbaud figure, scared of no one and ready for anything: "Jung rarely did anything directly, he always had a few vassals known for their life-and-death devotion to him. When he got drunk he would shoot at us with a revolver, like a cowboy in a wild-west film. . . . He was one of the most intelligent men I have ever met, but also one of the unhappiest."[15]

In November, 1918, Jung was active with "irregular" revolutionary forces, and by 1920 he was working on Agitprop dramas, which were published by Wieland Herzfelde's Communist-oriented Malik Verlag. The plays, *Die Kanaker* (The Cannibals) and *Wie lange noch?* (How Much Longer?) formed Volume II in the *Sammlung revolutionärer Bühnenwerke* (1921); and *Annemarie* (1922) was Volume XXI in the same series, which included political dramas by Erich Mühsam, Upton Sinclair, Karl August Wittfogel, Heinrich Stadelmann, and Felix Gasbarra. Jung's plays immediately attracted the attention of Erwin Piscator, who had opened Das proletarische Theater in Berlin on October 15, 1920. Piscator put on both *The Cannibals* and *How Much Longer? Annemarie*, which was planned for production in 1923/24, had to be abandoned for financial reasons. What attracted Piscator to Jung was obvious enough—he was looking for a means of making propaganda in the class war for the revolution. Inspired by the Russian Proletkult, he wanted to capture the present on the stage and record reality in order to show the discrepancy between things as they are and things as they ought to be:

The style, which actors and directors alike should master, must be absolutely concrete in nature (something like a Lenin or Chicherin manifesto, a style which in its simple, peaceful flow, and in its unmistakable clarity of meaning, exercises a powerful effect even at the purely emotive level). Whatever is said must be said in an unmannered, unexperimental, un-"*expressionistic*," unintense manner arrived at from the simple, plain, revolutionary aim and intention. Thereby all the Neo-Romantic, Expressionistic, or what-have-you styles and problems which stem from the individual anarchic needs of the bourgeois artist are eliminated right from the start.[16]

From this article in the *Gegner*, a journal which Jung edited, Piscator's anti-Expressionistic intention is quite clear, and yet Piscator himself realized that most of the revolutionary playwrights he was close to, including Jung himself, were still steeped in the style and concepts of Expressionism, although Jung had perhaps progressed furthest along the political path. This becomes particularly apparent from an examination of *How Much Longer?*

Whereas Toller still tended toward tragedy or at least toward dramas which showed the sensitive, idealistic protagonist in conflict with the world, Jung had moved on to a positive, proletarian standpoint in which the theater is a means to an end in the class struggle. He moved away from the abstract figures and dialectical confrontations, while at the same time avoiding the other pitfall of detailed Naturalism. Yet there are still indications of the Expressionist roots from which he comes, particularly in the use of music and the rhythmical structures for the scene sequences. The scenes themselves tend to be short and are interrupted by screams and sudden outbursts. Dramatic figures are often simply listed as First, Second, Third Worker; Wife; Girl; Bookkeeper; The Stranger; and Toller's satirical contrasts between the simplicity of the proletariat and the inflated

materialism of the bourgeoisie are still evident in Jung. Just
as Toller's *Masses and Man* culminates in a prison sequence
and a programmatic speech to the workers assembled in front
of the church, so too *How Much Longer?* has a dream sequence
followed by a long monologue spoken straight at the audience,
a speech characterized by the repeated longing for the Expressionist ideal of *Gemeinschaft*. The wife who is suddenly
on the stage beside the worker Paul, picked out in the light,
then develops the argument about violence or nonviolence already
familiar from Toller:

Wenn jemand Macht haben will, muss er mit Macht kämpfen. Geht
auf die Straße. Reisst die Fabriken an Euch. Arbeitet los: Wir
verhungern. Und macht, dass wir auch *glauben*, dass es Euch ernst
ist. Wir müssen das fühlen können. . . . Sonst glaub ich dir nicht.

(If anybody wants to have power, then he must fight with all his
might. Go into the streets. Seize the factories for yourselves. You
work. We starve. And make us believe you are in *earnest*. We have
to be able to feel that. . . .)[17]

Jung is writing in the postrevolutionary phase in the full
knowledge of the lack of unity within the working class itself,
and he constantly returns to this theme of solidarity. Here in
*How Much Longer?* the rebellion is easily put down, but Paul
the worker-hero is joined in his cell by another who is "dressed
exactly like him and has the same figure and face." This is his
comrade and brother, symbolizing, in truly Expressionistic manner, that the man of the masses is never alone. The final speech
spoken by this comrade raises yet again the Expressionist theme
of sacrifice.

Kopf hoch. Sieh dahin . . . (*Sie blicken jetzt beide ins Publikum*).
Wenn alle diese auch nur einen Funken gefasst haben, er wird
weiterglühen. Wir schleudern diesen Funken hinaus, wir, die noch
Opfer sind, in den Gefängnissen sitzen oder sonstwie zugrunde gehen.
Von unserer Kraft wird es abhängen, die Glut weiterzuschüren, den
Kopf hochzuhalten, und das Beispiel zu geben, an das die anderen
draussen sich klammern. Dann wächst von selbst draussen schon
der Bau hoch, in den wir ohne Ketten frei einziehen werden. Glaub
mir, sie werden daran arbeiten, nur du darfst nicht wanken.

(Head up. Look out there ... (*Both look straight into the audience*). If all of them have caught even one little spark, it will keep burning. We fling out these sparks, we who still make the sacrifices, sit in prisons or are ruined in some other way. It will depend on our strength to keep the fire going, keep our heads up, and give the example for the others outside to hold on to. Then the structure will grow by itself out there, for us to move into without chains as free men; only you must be steadfast.) [18]

This looking to the future, combined with the sacrifice and the leadership principle, is still very Expressionistic.

Jung's drama, *The Cannibals* (a proletarian drama in three acts), follows very much the same pattern as *How Much Longer?*—only at greater length. The title already indicates the message of the play, namely that the present state of society is marked by Kanakertum or cannibalism. Not only are different classes at war and trying to devour each other, but even within one and the same class the same lack of solidarity, the same cannibalism rages. Before the play starts, a brief prologue provides the universal framework. This little scene starts with a scream, as the curtain goes up and a man and woman are caught kissing, then the man comments on the two businessmen who can be seen, one American-style, the other a Europeanized Japanese:

Das sind die mit der Maschine. Sie streiten sich noch immer um die Maschine. Ich habe schon mal gehört. Die schrecken vor nichts zurück. Über die ganze Welt kommt Krieg und Hunger.

(They are the ones with the machine. They are still fighting about the machine. I've heard before. They'll stop at nothing. War and starvation are on the way for the whole world.) [19]

This passage in Expressionistic shorthand indicates that the particular incident that follows is only part of the worldwide machinations of international capitalism, which deliberately throttles production in one country in order to favor another.

In the second act of *The Cannibals*, the theme of the play is made explicit in a debate between two philosophers, described at first, in Expressionistic manner, as The Grey Man and The

Brown Man. When they remove their wigs and beards, they turn out to be Lenin and H. G. Wells. Here again, despite the rather pedestrian dialogue, the Expressionist manner breaks through, first of all in H. G. Wells, who develops Nietzsche-Darwinian ideas about the New Man, the survival of the fittest, and the need for racial selection. His is a vision of the new, hard, technocratic world which is emerging out of feudal capitalism. Then Lenin, too, falls into the Expressionist rhetoric in the lengthy monologue with which he counters this defense of cannibalism.

If the language of the play still sounds very close to Toller, the same is true of the nonlinguistic, visual and dramatic devices which Jung employs to further dramatically his cause of political agitation. Thus, Act I ends as follows, after a fire alarm and the sound of shots:

*Music starts up. First three drum beats in march tempo. Then wild march with crude instruments. Like circus music but not so sentimental. Noisily, partly out of tune, as if the instruments were moving away from each other. But the top melody has to be held, and the rhythm. The people in the stalls have to fly out of their seats. It must be impossible for them to whisper filthy jokes into each others' ears. The march gets wilder. Any attempt at criticizing the play becomes impossible. The march lasts five minutes. Ends with three drum beats. After that, like an echo, three bangs on the gong.*
*The curtain rises.*

As in Toller's plays, the tendency toward social criticism and attacks on bourgeois society is particularly marked, and like Toller, Jung underscores such scenes of satirical exposure with music. The whole of the last part of Act II has musical accompaniment, this time chamber, café, or cinema music "with melody and rhythm such as one hears for especially difficult variety acts, grotesque clowns, etc." The music has to accompany the action throughout, only breaking off suddenly at crucial points. The theatrical developments themselves have to flicker past at great speed, with jerky rhythm, giving the impression of "something unnatural, frantic, puppet-like, unreal," and most important of all, *"one should never for a moment be allowed to forget that these are actors acting to music."* This is a long way still from Piscator's ideal of proletarian realism and simplicity, and much closer to Kornfeld's theory of Expressionist acting. The plot of *The Cannibals* is painfully simple. The workers' revolt is spontaneous and unplanned. They take over the factory in a manner which has since become familiar in England and France, in the 1970's, and try to run it themselves. They put up no resistance when paramilitary forces are moved in and they are rounded up and shot.

Essentially the same situation is used by Jung in *Annemarie* (1922). The mine by this name is deliberately manipulated into financial trouble by the capitalists, thereby inducing confrontation with the workers. Once again there is the same cynical, ruthless behavior from the propertied classes and the same uncertainty and lack of solidarity among the workers. This play, too, ends with a catastrophe when the workers, surrounded by the police, are killed by a mine explosion. Here, too, Jung seems to be struggling with his Expressionist roots—there is ecstatic utterance, a vision, and a utopian epilogue after the catastrophe. But the attempt to move toward the collective, and the exposure of the economic forces governing the real world is laudable and is a definite step in the direction of Brecht, whose theory of the Gestus and of Historisieren Jung anticipated in his theoretical comments on this play.

After these three plays for Piscator, Jung went on to write *Legende* (Legend), *Heimweh* (Homesickness), and *Geschäfte* (Business), in which, to some extent, he returned once more to the stylistic devices of Expressionism, which is perhaps why Piscator, in his history of the Proletarian Theater, described them as "plays of dissolution, in which everything was based on vague gesture, fractured sentences and half words."[20] Jung remained in Berlin until 1937, involved in various scandals. He was one of the backers for Brecht's *Rise and Fall of the City of Mahagonny* and ran a dive called the Three Penny Cellar. In the Hitler years he fled to Prague, Vienna, Paris, and Geneva and ran a Swiss insurance agency in Hungary, before escaping to the United States, where he lived in New York and San Francisco. He died in Stuttgart in 1963, a lonely survivor from the age of Expressionism.

## V  *Johannes R. Becher*

Johannes R. Becher (1891–1958) was another Expressionist who survived. Famous for the role he played in East Berlin as Minister for Culture from 1954 on, he had been, in his time, one of the wildest of the ecstatic, "pathetic" poets of the Expressionist era. But where Jung always seemed to hover on the fringes of Communism without becoming a member of the party, Becher gradually moved from association with the Spartakusbund toward the end of the First World War into important positions in the party in the 1920's. He was, for example, one of the editors of the party journal *Linkskurve*. At first he still felt that the language and general style of Expressionism could be used for pacifist and pro-revolutionary propaganda, but he did, in the end, accept the party doctrine of Socialist Realism and became one of its strictest proponents. When forced to leave Germany in 1933, he moved by way of Prague, Vienna, and Paris to Moscow, where he remained till the end of the war. His career in Berlin and his association with Brecht after the war are well known.

Becher seems to have begun to take an interest in dramatic experiments as early as 1916. Unfortunately, of the various titles he mentions (which include the strikingly Expressionistic *Der neue Mensch!*) he seems to have completed only two, *Auftrieb* and *Hans im Glück*, apart from the Festspiel *Arbeiter Bauern Soldaten* (Workers Peasants Soldiers).[21] *Auftrieb* (Lift) and *Hans im Glück* (Lucky Jack) have been lost, and only the incomplete *Ikaros* remains, besides the first version of the Festspiel, to give some idea of what his early Expressionistic dramas were like. *Ikaros* is first mentioned by Becher in September, 1918, but between this date and the publication of the fragment in the yearbook *Die Erhebung* in 1919 came the November Revolution, the establishment of the Bavarian Republic, and the onset of counter-revolutionary reaction, events which are discernible in the published version. Hence, although the three characters of the play bear the classical names Icarus, Daedalus, and Heracles, the action takes place in the present and the costumes, stage design, and spirit of the play, with its burning confession of faith in a revolution which will bring all mankind freedom and liberation, are completely contemporary:

> Tausend Völker
> Verschlingen sich zu fabelhaftestem Bund.
> Die Kriege löschen aus. Vertilger wir der Morde.
> Erbsünde glüht aus. Wir büssten deutlich.
> Nun aber nennen wir uns einig Volk von Brüdern.
> Und menschlich, keusch und fromm solch Neuer Tag!

> (Thousands of peoples
> Join arms in the most fabulous of unions.
> Wars burn themselves out. We are destroyers of assassins.
> Original sin fades away. We made clear penance.
> Now we can call ourselves a united people of brothers.
> And human, chaste and pure such a New Day.)[22]

This may be a dream, as the father says, a dangerous drug, which has no place in reality, but it can also, as Ikaros claims, be a millenium worth striving for in the future, if man will have faith in himself, for man is not born of evil. Becher's faith is a political, not a religious one, namely: "Der Mensch ist gut!" (Man is good!).

In the five years between 1919 and 1924, Becher went through an extensive political development mirrored in the total rewriting of his Festspiel which, from having been "the departure of a people on its path to God," became a "revolutionary drama of struggle." He abandoned his earlier drawing-room Communism with its confused and ecstatic quest for God, once he had come to realize that only active revolution could change society and bring about the "realm of humanity"—his goal from the start. Both plays still operate with nameless figures, and the background to the action is still the November Revolution. In both, living conditions are unbearable, and someone comes forward to express the longing for release of the oppressed and the despairing and to urge revolt. But in the second version, the direction is entirely different—instead of aimlessness there is now a direct appeal to the soldiers of the revolutionary, class-conscious proletariat urging them to fight. In the 1919 version, the Man (a poet) is the leader of the masses, and millions gather around him. At the front, a Woman appeals to the soldiers to refuse to fight, and all follow this lead including general and tyrant. But when the Woman is shot, chaos breaks out. Part Three brings the march of the workers, peasants, and soldiers, through the sandy wilderness "toward the miracle." The suffering people join them, the tyrant abandons his throne, the rich give up their wealth, and even the audience joins this united brotherhood of man in its joyful march into the promised land.

In the 1924 version, this kind of elevated biblical language is rejected, the style becomes concrete and hard and socio-economic reasons are given where possible. There is still an army of millions, but now it assembles from the factories and workplaces, and the Man and Woman join the masses, instead of the other way around. Seeking refuge in God is denounced as weakness; instead, action for revolutionary change is called for. The situation at the front is shown upon news of the creation of soldiers' councils, and the intrigues of the officers to divert the revolution are unmasked. The revolutionary woman leader tries to warn the soldiers, but the officers gain control of the revolution, and she is put into prison. Here, in a monologue quoting Liebknecht's "Trotz alledem!" she proclaims her faith in the victory of the working classes. Meanwhile, among the officers the assassination of Rosa Luxemburg and Karl Lieb-knecht is being planned. The moral for the audience is put across by two workers who discuss the reasons for their defeat: the workers must learn and organize! What then follows is the complete abandonment of dramatic dialogue in the notorious German Cesspool sequence:

Guidelines for the presentation of the German Cesspool. In this part there is a great deal of work with the spot-lighting; so, first one, then another group moves into the foreground. This part is to be played as a political fairground, as circus act. Especially here widest scope should be left to the imagination of the actors. Cabaret songs, Swastika dances, loud shouts of Sieg Heil. Genuinely patriotic orgies. Following the motto, the bigger the crook, the bigger the swine, the more he acts like a patriot. Everything is possible here. Ghastliest tales of Jewish horrors, about how they have a League for the Establishment of Jewish World Supremacy, etc., etc. Everything anarchic, mechanical, automaton-like in the capitalistic system is to be brought out. . . .[23]

This continues for some pages. After the German Cesspool, workers, peasants, soldiers in all the countries of the world revolt. Their march is joined by representatives of various social classes and in recitatives and choruses they speak and sing the "Great Red Marching Anthem." This vision concluded with a dedication to the German Communist comrade.

The difference between the later and the earlier Becher, and between Becher and Toller, is now clearly demonstrated. The radical rejection of war combined with out-and-out pacifism is now confronted with the realities of the November Revolution and after. The mission of the poet as leader by reason of the power of the spirit is abandoned as illusory, and the new man emerges not by miraculous revelation but through revolutionary conflict. As Becher had witnessed in postwar Germany, the different classes had not come together into a harmonious union of mankind; instead, class divisions had become more than ever marked and class *conflict* had to be accepted as the only means of change. In the Festspiel, Becher had shared the common Expressionist longing for *Gemeinschaft*, but like so many Expressionists he had not been able to see any way to bring about this ideal of harmony and brotherhood. All he could offer was a visionary dream of utopian equality in freedom from war and exploitation. By the time he remodeled his Festspiel into a "revolutionary drama of conflict," he had accepted the historical role of the working class in the struggle for humanism. Thus, his work became a sober call to arms, couched not in ecstatic rhetoric, but in a new laconic style which points to the later Brechtian Lehrstücke.

However, the really striking feature of the revised work is the move in the direction of the revolutionary pageant with mass choruses, marches, and speeches. As in Russian Proletkult, theater is taking to the streets. Becher made the point clearly enough in the "Remark on the Revision":

It is part of the play that, for example, revolutionary pamphlets are distributed before the start, that groups form for discussions, that speeches should be made, that the actors should first march through the city to the theater, arranged in columns, with bands, red flags, drawings, posters, banners etc. All this should organize itself spontaneously. Professional actors are only admissible in so far as they subordinate themselves to the whole. No stars....[24]

Becher then marks the extreme reaction to the events of the November Revolution. Toller, as has been seen, lived through it and recorded in *Masses and Man* the tragedy of the revolutionary who was guilty if he resorted to force and guilty if he did not. Hasenclever showed with his play, *Die Entscheidung* (The Decision), that he had lost faith in the revolution. Becher did not see the situation as tragic and never lost his faith in the ultimate victory of the working class. In June, 1925, for his works, *Am Grabe Lenins* (By Lenin's Grave), *Vorwärts du rote Front* (Forward You Red Front), *Der Leichnam auf dem Thron* (The Corpse on the Throne), and for the revolutionary drama, *Workers Peasants Soldiers*, a case was brought against him. On the basis of one sentence from the play: "In this republic only the rich are allowed to plunder," he was accused of an offense against the state and of sowing the seeds of high treason. The early Becher, the ecstatic poet notorious for his dabbling in drugs and sex, was gone, and his place had been taken by a very political animal, capable of giving considerable disquiet in "right-thinking quarters."

## VI   *Friedrich Wolf*

But for all his later fame, his association with Brecht and the Theater am Schiffbauerdamm, Becher is not thought of primarily as a man of the theater. The leading revolutionary dramatist, who, like him, rose to high office in the German Democratic Republic, was Friedrich Wolf (1888–1953).[25] Wolf was a dramatist who attained world fame, particularly in the post-Expressionist period with his realistic treatment of contemporary social problems. His *Cyankali* (Potassium Cyanide [1929]), in which a girl dies of an abortion, was his most sensational success; *The Sailors of Cattaro* (1930) has already been mentioned as an example of a revolutionary play in a

Navy setting; while *Professor Mamlock* (1934), the story of a Jewish surgeon who is driven to suicide by Nazi persecution, swept around the world in its time not only as a play but as a brilliant film. Plays of this kind were not only sensationally and scandalously successful, they brought down the wrath of reactionary government upon his head.

Since his successes of the 1920's and 1930's, Wolf's dramas have been practically forgotten outside the German Democratic Republic, where he is revered as a classic; and even there his early work from the Expressionist period has tended to be ignored in favor of the later works of Socialist Realism. Yet, as with Becher and Brecht, there is no doubt that he has his roots deep in Expressionism. After qualifying as a doctor, he served in the army in the First World War, an experience which turned him into an ardent pacifist. In 1919 he became a member of the Workers and Soldiers Council in Dresden, was imprisoned for participating in a demonstration against the assassination of Karl Liebknecht and Rosa Luxemburg, and was arrested subsequently for his play *Potassium Cyanide*. By this time he was very much a political person, although he did not become a member of the Communist Party until 1928. Denounced as an enemy of the people, he was forced to leave Germany in 1933 on Hitler's rise to power and did not return until 1945 having, like Brecht, spent the intervening years in exile (in his case in Switzerland, France, Scandinavia, the United States, but mainly in the Soviet Union).

Wolf's earliest literary works show distinct traces of his reading—Schopenhauer, Nietzsche, and Tolstoy's doctrine of non-aggression and pacifism. His very first play *Mohammed* was "written in the trenches of Flanders in the summer of 1917" and is a characteristically Expressionistic work, rich in monologues and visions yet lacking in dramatic action or plot.[26] Mohammed is the leader who gradually breaks through to a realization and acceptance of his own true path. Other Expressionist dramas followed—*Das bist Du* (That's You [1919]); *Der Unbedingte* (Absolute Man [1919]); his first comedy *Die schwarze Sonne* (The Black Sun. A Fantastic Comedy with Singing and Dancing [1920]); and *Tamar*, written in 1921 in Worpswede, where he had joined a socialist commune. None of these plays could be described as realistic, but in *Absolute Man* at least there are the beginnings of a systematic treatment of class conflict and of acceptance of the role of the proletariat.

The most important event in Wolf's Expressionist period, however, was the production of *That's You* in the revolutionary Dresden of 1919. This was the first of Wolf's plays to reach the stage, and the production of Berthold Viertel with sets by the artist Conrad Felixmüller was a sensational triumph for the Expressionist style.[27] Wolf had a clear idea of what he wanted to put across. The basic spiritual and dramatic principle was the idea that all existence is a constant flux, that man, too—especially man—is in a state of constant transformation from the lower forms to the higher. At that time, he had still read no Hegel or Marx and was steeped in Schopenhauer and in the teachings of the ancient philosophy of the Vedas. Human existence had to pass through many different stages, but everywhere, everything one passes through: "tat twam asi!" (That is you!). With one foot in the purgatory of the First World War, that is how he saw the problem of the responsibility of the individual: each man is responsible not merely for himself but also for everybody else! Any one failure contributes to the failure of others.

This was the basic idea of the play. The task of the artist Felixmüller was to translate it into visual effects. Felixmüller had worked before with Erich Ziegel, the director of the Hamburg Kammerspiele, doing stage designs for Kornfeld's *Seduction* where he demonstrated his principle of breaking down the rigid walls of the proscenium arch, using movable props in place of fixed sets and changing them with the curtain up. The basic conception of *That's You* lent itself to this kind of treatment. The prologue and the epilogue had, as it were, prenatal and postmortal "beings"; in the play itself these beings appear in action as good, solid citizens. But in the prologue and the epilogue they flit from star to star. Felixmüller solved this difficult problem by putting the actors into rigid starched canvas costumes, against a cubistic space made of lateral lines in front of an arching horizon. He had numerous arc lights shining upward on them from below. At the same time, with the lights from below and from the wings he could constantly change the spaces into a tiny little pointed star, a flattened box, a plane stretching into infinity, etc.

Dramatically and scenically the most important part, however, was the central part of the play, which was a down-to-earth, very realistic story about three men and a woman. An apprentice gardener is incited by a blacksmith to seduce the wife of the head gardener so that the apprentice can revenge himself on his boss. The young man resists for a long time until one night the two young people fall asleep under the spell of the moon. And now in their dream the objects in the room begin to act out a life of their own: the crucifix as a Cross of Christ, the hatchet as a murder weapon, the couch on which they both lie as an evil woman bringing them together. Felixmüller had to express this scenically. He solved the problem magnificently, and in a simple and fascinating way. The walls of the room, the coverings of the couch and of a second (much larger) ax were transparent. And suddenly, while the light in the young couple's dream fades, the moon starts to come in through the wall, the "faces" of the crucifix, the couch, the ax start their debate as to where these two lovers and dreamers belong. As the room dissolves into nothing, the two people sleep on in an infinite landscape beneath a gigantic moon surrounded by the conflicting spirits of the objects.

Reading the play today it is difficult to recapture the excitement of these revolutionary days in Dresden. In the play, the alternation between real and twilight world seems fragile and confused, yet there is no doubt from contemporary reports that this was a case where author, director and stage director combined to produce the kind of stage magic that was the aim of the whole Expressionist movement in the theater. Like Felixmüller, who went on to become a powerful Realist and portrayer of the class struggle, Wolf could also build on these beginnings to develop into one of the most effective revolutionary dramatists of his time.

## CHAPTER 6

# Religion and Ecstasy:
## Lautensack, Kornfeld, Werfel, Einstein, Jahn, Brust, Bronnen

### I  *Expressionism and Religion*

IF it is easy to dismiss Expressionist politics as empty enthusiasm without awareness of what is possible in the real
world, it has proved equally easy to accuse many leading
Expressionists of lacking reason and logic in their religious attitudes. But just as Expressionist politics turn out to be not as
naive as they appear at first sight, so, too, the religious aspirations
of the Expressionists are often not only understandable but
defensible on closer examination.[1] Unfortunately, they do need
some defense because, in their religious quest, the Expressionists
regularly strayed from the paths of orthodoxy and, especially in
their dramatic works, often gave much greater offense than
they had ever done by their most outré treatment of the problems
of war and revolution. Expressionist religious drama gave rise
to one theatrical scandal after another.

However, the fact that the Expressionists were fundamentally
religious will be readily accepted. What they were clearly re-
acting against was a certain kind of arid materialism, and what
they favored was a life-style which would offer something deep
and significant. Instead of the Here and the Now, they sought
the Eternal and the Absolute; they demanded a metaphysical
world view, a new religion, not just a solution to economic, social,
and political problems, but the salvation of mankind. In this
light it may seem paradoxical that they should put so much
stress on *man*: indeed, compounds of *Mensch* and *Menschheit*
are key concepts for the whole of Expressionism. What they

meant, however, was not man in a physical sense. Man must become true to himself. "Mensch werde wesentlich!" the words of Angelus Silesius quoted by Stadler, become almost a motto for Expressionism. Man as created by God must strive to realize his full potential. This meant a rejection of psychology as a purely rational science which attempted to explain man's behavior in terms of certain conditioning factors in the mind. For the Expressionists, man was not restricted and confined by the conscious or unconscious limitations of the mind; he was a creature with a soul, which was not subject to causal laws. Man was free to experience a revelation, and hence, a total transformation, from one second to the next.

Not surprisingly, in view of this receptivity for spiritual insights, Strindberg's religious plays like *To Damascus* and the *Dream Play* provide the models; and even an early play like Sorge's *The Beggar* (1910) shows the essentially religious nature of Expressionist drama. The young protagonist of that play is a poet, but his role in life is "to speak through symbols of eternity." The role of the artist is viatic, and the poet sees himself as a prophet-leader showing mankind the true path: this mission is an essentially religious one. Linked with this mission is the possibility of salvation, both as something ardently to be desired, but also as something ultimately attainable, however vague and *schwärmerisch* the expressed longings may appear. Barlach, for example, is a God-seeker; and Stefan Zweig, in a play like *Jeremiah*, shows the same kind of prophetic religiosity, the same monumental style. Kokoschka, too, is a fundamentally religious writer, and one is not surprised to find specifically religious titles among his works like *The Burning Bush* and *Job*.

It is tempting at this point to look for the roots of this metaphysical religious attitude among the German philosophers of irrationalism, or even in the continuing strain of German mysticism from Johann Tauler and Heinrich Suso in the Middle Ages to Jakob Böhme and others in subsequent centuries. The Expressionists were certainly aware of the mystics and claimed them as their spiritual ancestors. On the other hand, Plato's nearness to the myth and Socrates' question-and-answer quest for ultimate truth have also been named among metaphysical models for the age. Nor was this generation limited to the

Western world. One of the most striking features of Expressionism was the influence of Eastern thought. In his essay, "The Doctrine of Tao," Martin Buber spoke about the mother principle as distinct from the father principle as a basic religious attitude, and Lao Tse became such a fashionable phenomenon that there was a whole wave of translations from the Chinese about this time. He is constantly being mentioned and discussed by Expressionist poets and critics, and verses from the *Taoteking* are often quoted. Nearer to hand than China, however, there was also the very powerful influence of Swedenborg. Sometimes his is only a shadowy presence, but in a dramatist like Hasenclever his impact was direct and lasting. Always he is used as a weapon against the intellectuality and logic of a Kant and as a living demonstration of the primeval forces of the soul, intuition, and the unconscious.

Appealing to such forces could mean unleashing those of chaos, and this the Expressionists almost wilfully did. Order was felt to be sterile and chaos fruitful. Not surprisingly, the idealization of chaos and the chaotic as the source of life meant that the drama produced by the Expressionists often seemed to lack order, apart from being morally offensive. But this was only a reflection of the will for cosmic dynamism in the hope that, from the mighty sparks that were being struck, some great revelation would emerge. At its worst, this could be disastrous for the drama; at its best, when chaos was fashioned and led into formal channels, the tension produced could be overwhelming. The Expressionist was not being loud and pathetic because he was an empty shell with nothing to express: he preferred the grand gesture, the pathos, because he felt compelled to penetrate to the mysteries of existence. If this meant shouting and rhapsodic utterance, then so be it; for such ecstasy would be a religious experience bringing the recipient of the vision nearer to ultimate truth.

## II  *The Drama of Transfiguration*

Expressionist dramas have been called *Wandlungsdramen*, and the drama of transfiguration or metamorphosis is certainly one of the preferred forms of the period. The transformation is more readily demonstrated through before-and-after phases. For example, in Kaiser's *From Morn till Midnight*, the cashier is, at the beginning, reduced to a mere function, a machine for counting money, until through the touch of an exotic Italian woman he is almost literally switched on, comes to life for the first time, and sets out on his quest for his soul and for ultimate values. Stories of this kind were common at the time: indeed, one of Kafka's most famous stories is *Die Verwandlung* (The Metamorphosis). But it is the dramatic, rather than the narrative, form which proves the most effective vehicle for demonstrating the transformation. The quest on which the protagonist of the drama embarks is generally not a successful one, and for this reason it has become customary to insinuate that the Expressionists had no very useful message to offer.

Yet they cannot be dismissed as merely utopian, because the vision of a better world *was* something for the age in which they lived. They were not practical men offering practical solutions; they were visionaries, and proud of it. And what was their vision? Kaiser summed it up in one lapidary sentence: "There is only one: the vision of the regeneration of man." There is a paradise ahead, a golden age when there will be no false distinctions between men, a classless society beyond politics, attainable through the ideal of brotherhood. Then there will be no more evil, no more violence, no more wars. Man is good; he has simply so far failed to allow his goodness to unfold to the full. The world can be changed but not by any means other than by the advent of the New Man.

## III    *Heinrich Lautensack*

Whether Heinrich Lautensack (1881–1919) can, with any justification, be classified as an Expressionist is doubtful, but he does, without question, belong in a chapter devoted to religion and ecstasy. As in Wedekind, whom he worshipped next to idolatry, the central theme of all of Lautensack's work is love of the kind he himself called "sexual."[2] While, in many respects, Lautensack seems more an exponent of the *Volksstück* than of avant-garde experimental drama, his literary career nevertheless shows many points of contact with Expressionism. He published in Expressionist journals like *Die Aktion,* which also discussed his notorious collection of poems, *Dokumente der Liebesraserei* (*Documents of Love's Madness* [1919]), and recommended it only to very tough-minded readers. His *Via crucis* was published in another Expressionist series, the Bücherei Maiandros, in December, 1912, together with a lithograph of a crucifixion by Max Beckmann. At an early stage, he was associated with cabaret through the famous Elf Scharfrichter and with the beginnings of cinematography; indeed, he must have been one of the first scriptwriters. Lautensack built up a reputation as a bohemian literary gypsy and "Satanist of Eroticism,"[3] but despite all his artistic contacts in the big city he never seems to have lost his longing for his beloved Bavarian countryside, and it is when he writes of Bavaria in his plays that he is at his best.

Lautensack's play, *Medusa* (1904), is too early to be Expressionistic in any way. It is a treatment of a sexual theme, that of the ugly girl who longs for a love that will be higher than mere physical contact. Lautensack's next play, a comedy called *Hahnenkampf* (Cock Fight [1910]), brought him into the first of his many conflicts with the censor. As a result, there is more than one version of the text, including an extra scene published in *Die Aktion.* The plot of this comedy is quite simple: Innocentia, the girl, belongs to a group of local dignitaries in an unnamed township in Bavaria. When a new gendarme arrives, they all get a little worried for their good name, especially when Innocentia and the gendarme fall in love, and he threatens to bring a case against them unless they release her from her sexual bondage to them. In the end, the gendarme is killed and his murder is covered up as suicide. Because of its theme it was ten years before this play could be performed.

In the same way, Lautensack's most successful work for the stage, *Die Pfarrhauskomödie* (Vicarage Comedy [1911]), had to wait for the abolition of censorship after the war before becoming one of the most exciting theatrical events of the twenties. In Hanover it could only be performed with special security police in the theater; in Hagen there was a special performance for the trade unions; in Berlin it enjoyed a long run after much trouble, interrupted performances, customers demanding their money back, law suits, etc. The play was performed all over Germany and drew comments ranging from pure praise to one out-and-out condemnation of it as the "foetus born of a crazed brain and a shameless imagination."[4]

All Lautensack had done was to deal very humorously and realistically with the ancient theme of the celibacy of the priest. The action takes place in a country parsonage between four sinners. The priest's cook, Ambrosia, is leaving at the beginning to have her baby elsewhere. A replacement cook, Irma, arrives. She knows the truth and insists on making those around her see the truth as well. In particular, she makes the priest's assistant, Vincenz, see what is happening, and using the priest as an excuse, she makes Vincenz aware of his own manhood and natural human desires. Vincenz even experiences an Expressionistic rebirth and becomes a New Man:

VINCENZ:  (*Drinks. That's to say he drinks even more beer.*) I've become a different person! I've become young! Young! I've become younger! I'd have gone old—but for you! Drink!
(*They both drink.*)
IRMA:     You've become a new man!

By the end she, too, is pregnant, but, as a final twist, she manages to make the priest think that he may be the father and so blackmails him into finding a living for the assistant, so that he will be able to support her.

Lautensack's play *Das Gelübde* (The Vow [1916]) also combined sex and religion in a manner that was to become almost the trademark of the Expressionist play. It was first published by René Schickele in *Die weissen Blätter* and then appeared in book form with Kurt Wolff in 1916. The action of the play takes place before the outbreak of hostilities. Pater Felix, formerly Count Horst von Hilgartsberg, has entered a monastery and taken an oath of chastity. After some years he is told that his wife, whom he has believed dead in a shipwreck, has been alive all the time, has lived in an Arab harem, and is on her way back to Germany. On her return, the potentially comic situation becomes tragic when a real conflict develops between the oath he has sworn and her marital rights as a wife. In the end, she makes the great sacrifice and, following church law, she, too, takes the oath of chastity and enters a nunnery. The high point of the play is reached in Act III, when, as in Kornfeld's play, *The Seduction*, the wife attempts with all her womanly charms to seduce her husband and fails.

Like the North German Barlach, Lautensack always gave his works a firm foundation in the peasant reality of his homeland before moving into his grotesque situations, and a certain discrepancy between setting and production could result when his works were transferred to the stage. This was the case with the first performance of *The Vow*. The audience knew that Lautensack's Batau was really Passau; the hotel, monastery, and nunnery were easily identifiable as real places; but the stage design by Paris von Gütersloh was completely Expressionistic and unreal. Nevertheless, the first-night audience seems to have been gripped by the play and burst into spontaneous applause at the end of the third act. The fourth act, which had caused the author a great deal of trouble and rewriting, received a very mixed response, and this was reflected in the fighting that broke out in the theater. Yet there is no doubt whatsoever that Lautensack was himself a devout person who never intended, in this or any other of his plays, simply to create a scandal or give offense. As Herbert Ihering put it, "The curious thing is that Lautensack, although he can never get away from literary sources, has created a completely unliterary, religious, devout work. Devout in a church sense without subjection to any dogma, devout in the sense of being aware of the world without simply accepting liberalizing tendencies, devout in its belief in mankind through the total acceptance of humour."[5]

Lautensack's *The Vow* continued to be successfully performed, though on occasion without the controversial fourth act, and was also made into a very successful film. However, it is *The Vicarage Comedy* which has remained a firm favorite to this day, enjoying successful revivals in the 1970's like the comedies of Hermann Essig (1878–1918), whose comic Volksstücke also had similar difficulties with the censor.

## IV  *Paul Kornfeld*

One of the most influential dramatists of the Expressionist generation and one considered by his contemporaries to show the greatest promise was Paul Kornfeld (1889–1942). Born in Prague into a Jewish family of noted Talmudic scholars, Kornfeld moved to Germany where he became a dramaturg first with Reinhardt, in Berlin, then in the Hessisches Landestheater, Darmstadt. He also had a close association with Carl Zeiss, the theater director. It is perhaps particularly important to establish Kornfeld's theatrical credentials right from the start, because the two plays from his Expressionist period, *Die Verführung* (The Seduction) and *Himmel und Hölle* (Heaven and Hell), represent such a total rejection of all the accepted traditions of stage realism and psychological probability, that the unwary reader could be tempted to conclude that they must have been written by someone with no practical knowledge of the stage whatsoever. After these two Expressionist plays, Kornfeld, like many of his contemporaries, turned to stage comedy. He left Germany in 1933 and returned to Prague, where he worked for many years on a novel, *Blanche oder Das Atelier im Garten* (Blanche or the Studio in the Garden). In 1941 he was arrested and removed to the extermination camp at Lodz, where he is presumed to have died in January 1942. Today his Expressionist plays are never performed, but his famous essay, "Der beseelte oder der psychologische Mensch" (Psychological Man or Man with a Soul), published in the first number of *Das junge Deutschland* (1918), is still read as the most radical statement of Expressionist dramatic art.

Paul Kornfeld wrote his first tragedy, *The Seduction*, in 1913. In May, 1916, he added an "Epilogue to the Actor," and the work was accepted for publication in that year by S. Fischer. The first edition appeared in 1917, and by 1921 five editions in all had appeared, a fact which by itself indicates how seriously the play was taken by critics and general public alike. The première took place in December, 1917, in Frankfurt am Main, under the direction of Hans Hartung, with Jakob Feldhammer as male protagonist. The leading lady, Fritta Brod, later became Kornfeld's wife. By all accounts, this première was a considerable success and was reckoned to be one of the most important events of the theatrical season. Julius Bab, the critic, treated it at the time as one of the most significant examples of the new Expressionist drama, while Kasimir Edschmid, looking back on the event in his memoirs, wrote:

The leading lady was Fritta Brod, a slim, blond, lily-like actress, almost incorporeal, all spirituality in the language, clearly only born for the purpose of acting in Kornfeld's plays, which were more spoken operas than dramas. . . . Fritta Brod was of a poetic abstraction exactly matching Kornfeld's abstract drama, the plot of which was often ridiculous, the inner content being unraveled only with the help of endless monologues—though it must be admitted, that on the spiritual level the tension developed magnificently. But in the long run this was doubtless hardly bearable. After all Kornfeld had totally banished action from the drama, although he was convinced that he had brought a totally new and unbelievable inner activity to life in his plays. . . .
  Kornfeld's experiment was naturally, even as he intended it, magnificent, but simply not repeatable and in the long run turned into something far from magnificent. He was not made of iron like Kaiser (in his abstractness), he was abstract out of poetry.[6]

This comment by Edschmid is important because it success-fully isolates the reasons, both for Kornfeld's significance in his own time, and for the lack of interest in his work since then. Incorporeal spirituality and poetic abstraction were much ad-mired in the age of Expressionism, while ridiculous plots, spoken operas, and endless poetic monologues have not proved the key to success since then. Kornfeld is the extreme example of the earlier spiritual wing of Expressionism, with Strindberg, Dostoyevsky, and Wedekind clearly discernible as the spiritual roots of his work. A brief summary of the plot of *The Seduction* gives some idea of what Kornfeld confronted his audience with.

His drama has five acts, each of which marks a particular stage in the development of the action. In the first act the life of the hero, Bitterlich, is shown in its normal setting. The first of the stations on his path through life is a social call, which he pays with his mother. Here the milieu is petty bourgeois, characterized by soullessness and lack of under-standing; and the triviality of the life he encounters so disgusts

Bitterlich, especially as represented (as he sees it) by the soul-less philistine behavior of the fiancé toward the daughter of the house, that he simply strangles the man on the spot. He is arrested and taken to prison.

The second act shows him, still accompanied by his mother, in prison, where he insists on staying, although the prison governor and the attorney prove to be incredibly sensitive and understanding and offer him the means of escape. To attain complete isolation he banishes the dreamlike female figures that appear from his past and in the end even banishes his mother. However, in the third act Bitterlich submits to thoughts of external freedom; it is now that the "seduction" takes place. The girl Ruth wins him back for the world by making him see the possibilities of happiness and life. With unexpected help from his mother, who suddenly throws money over the wall, the escape from the prison is accomplished.

In Act IV, Bitterlich and Ruth join in a crude local celebration (a *Schweineschlachtfest*) at a village inn, until Ruth's brother is able to entice the pair back to town despite the mother's warnings. The falseness of the brother's promises are revealed at the end of this act, and Ruth and Bitterlich discover the brother's plan to use poison on Bitterlich. At the beginning of Act V, Ruth and the mother, the two women who love Bitterlich so much, try to foil the poison plan but fail. Bitterlich, although already poisoned, does not know this and persuades the brother to commit suicide by shooting himself. Once Ruth realizes that she has failed to save Bitterlich's life, she, too, takes the same poison that has killed him, and the play ends with the death of both Bitterlich and Ruth and the plaintive words of the mother who is now the only one left alive: "It was *my* son that died."

Clearly, Kornfeld seems to have gone out of his way to exaggerate the improbable elements in his plot. This is a play punctuated by strangling, shooting, and poisoning, in fact, all the ingredients of the most rubbishy melodrama—so much so indeed that it becomes clear that these excessively trivial and improbable elements are meant to demonstrate the complete un-importance of the external action. Everything is done to reinforce this impression; Bitterlich's girlfriends, Lotte and Leonore, simply walk into his prison cell without any explanation of how this can be possible; characters indulge in frequent asides and long soliloquies; while obvious lies reinforce the total absurdity of what is happening.

Moreover, Kornfeld is not content merely to stress the improbability and absurdity of events in the "real" world; he also feels compelled to diminish all visual, theatrical distractions as well. For him the stage is superfluous. As Kasimir Edschmid put it, "gramophones behind the scene would produce the same effect."[7] However, this is not merely lack of talent or ignorance of stagecraft: there is a deeper significance behind it all. His aim is to make the action transparent, so that the audience will see through the surface action to what is going on at that other, deeper level of the soul. More than half of the text consists of monologues. Language is the medium of Kornfeld's art; the language register shows immediately whether a person has a soul, a "fate" or not; language demonstrates the confrontation between those possessed of a soul and the soulless; language demonstrates the union of two souls when, for example, in the seduction scene in Act III, the voices of Ruth and Bitterlich soar upward together in linguistic harmony. This is the climax of the whole play, and as in an opera the protagonists are completely stationary. Ruth's death, too, is transported into the sphere of music:

Ah, wenn man liebt, soll man schweigen; wenn man stirkt soll man schweigen! Und nur Musik! Ich wollte, ich wäre ein tausendstimmiges Orchester—die Welt müsste erdröhnen unter meinen Melodien!

(Ah, when you're in love, you should remain silent; when you're dying, you should remain silent! And music alone! I wish I were an orchestra of a thousand—the world would have to thunder to my melodies!)[8]

She then sings a song before dying.

Altogether what this play demonstrates is the Expressionistic quest for the absolute—ecstasy, intensity of feeling, total surrender in love, utter despair at the world, complete maternal sacrifice. Regrettably, what appealed to the Expressionist generation is exactly what makes the play so indigestible now.

Bitterlich is described as crazy, a "fool," but at the same time he is held up by Kornfeld as an exceptional person, different from normal men in the day-to-day world, because he has a soul. Normal men have no fate, no soul; Bitterlich does have a soul, and indeed one filled with vast inner movement marked by the awareness of chaos. Such an experience is held to be identical with elemental, true, essential existence, for in a state of chaos these creative possibilities of man which are denied to utilitarian lives can unfold. Hence, there is no psychological motivation for Bitterlich's actions; he simply follows the dictates of his soul, which, by definition, is beyond logic or reason.

That Bitterlich has a soul is demonstrated, too, by his ability to suffer. Bitterlich relishes suffering; he does not avoid it, but on the contrary he tries to augment it. He deliberately seeks the suffering of the saint and martyr, so that others will worship him. Even for contemporary audiences this was going too far, and despite the combination of sex and soul which the title, *The Seduction*, promised, the audiences, after their initial fascination, stayed away. The seduction, after all, was more of an "Entführung" than a "Verführung"—Bitterlich is enticed out of the isolation of the prison into the world outside; he is never really seduced.

Bitterlich, then, is possessed of a soul; in Kornfeld's words he is "beseelt," and this soul explodes amidst crude village festivities, in the middle of singing, sex, and drunkenness. But when he attempts to embrace this world, he is rejected by it and laughed at.[9] There is clearly a religious message here, though it is not very well expressed. Further, it must be admitted that if the religious message of the play is not entirely clear, the morality seems to be deliberately offensive. The Chinese motto from Lao Tse which Kornfeld has given to the play includes the line: "Between good and evil: what difference is there?"; and throughout, the dramatist indulges in attacks on bourgeois morality.

That Kornfeld fails to be as offensive as he clearly intends to be can only be because the deliberately banal plot makes it impossible to take anything or anybody seriously—even the tragic outcome, brought about by the grotesque switch of two little bottles, one of which contains poison and the other urine.

Grotesque is a word which is frequently used in the play, and it can be applied particularly to Bitterlich's tragic end whereby, before he dies, he manages to persuade the philistine Wilhelm to shoot himself, a solution which is even more incredible than the manner of his own death. The important thing to realize, however, is that Kornfeld was fully aware of what he was doing, that he was creating this kind of play deliberately, as his "Epilogue to the Actor" makes clear: "I do not know whether this play will ever be presented on the stage. It has been written for the theater. If it is never produced I am prepared to accept any reason except one: namely that its style is not good theater."[10] This epilogue, which was later incorporated in the more extended essay, "Psychological Man and Man with a Soul," then goes on to develop the idea of *unnatural* production and *unnatural* action, culminating in the comparison with opera:

Let him therefore abstract from the attributes of reality and be nothing but a representative of thought, feeling or fate!

The melody of a great gesture says more than the highest consummation of what is called naturalness.

Let him think of the opera, in which the dying singer still gives forth a high C and with the sweetness of his melody tells more about death than if he were to crawl and writhe. For it is more important to know that death is anguish than that it is horrible.[11]

Kornfeld's second Expressionist play, *Heaven and Hell*, a tragedy, was completed and published in 1919. Graf Umgeheuer (a name almost identical with the word Ungeheuer, or monster) is unhappily married to Beate. All that remains between them after many years of matrimony is politeness and consideration for the other. Umgeheuer finds it difficult to say a good or kind word to her: at one point, for example, she has observed him through the keyhole and seen him weeping over a picture of her, but when she comes into the room with arms outstretched to embrace him, he screams at her to go. The count loves the prostitute, Maria, and to have her close he takes her into his house as his wife's maid. Maria, however, becomes fond of Beate and tries to bring the couple together again. To this end, she deliberately shows herself in an unfavorable light to the count and a reconciliation does come about between Beate and her husband.

But happiness is not to last very long. The count's daughter, Esther, is strangled by her mother, Beate, because she has failed to return her love. Maria wants to take the blame for the murder, but Beate insists that she is the guilty one. The two women fight over who should be punished for the crime. Then along comes Johanna, who is closely attached to Maria and wants to appear with her before the court. The marchioness, the countess's mother, argues that, in that case, she will have to have committed a crime, too, and so Johanna stabs the soulless marchioness. Beate confesses to her husband that it was she who committed the murder. Now he can love her; all the barriers that separate them crumble.

Meanwhile, Johanna and Maria are accused of murder and, as in so many Expressionist dramas, a courtroom scene follows, allowing the dialectic of the moral possibilities to be worked out in public discussion. Maria is quite happy to accept the death penalty; Johanna, however, still clings to life. Maria pleads on her behalf. Johanna also tries to help Maria and reveals that it was Beate who committed the murder. But the judge pronounces sentence of death on both of them. They accept the sentence gladly, and Beate also dies, ecstatically praising the value of suffering. In the epilogue, the count appears as a wanderer mourning in the desert. Johanna, Beate, and Maria descend on a cloud to fetch him to a higher realm:

DIE DREI TOTEN FRAUEN: Keine Seele ist verloren,
Jeder Mensch ist auserwählt
Jeder Mensch ist auserkoren,
Trotz Teufeln und Dämonen,
Dass er dem Göttlichen sich vermählt!
So schweben wir, schweben wir, schweben wir auf,
Unsterbliche Seelen, unsterblich in Äonen!

(*Sie entschweben mit dem Grafen*)
(*Jakob bleibt aufrecht stehen*)

(THE THREE DEAD WOMEN: No soul is lost,
         Every one is chosen
         Every one is elected
         Despite devils and demons,
         To wed the Divine!
         So we go soaring, soaring, soaring
          upwards,
         Immortal souls, immortal in æons
          of time!
*(They soar away upward with the count. Jakob remains standing.)* [12]

Although only about half the size of *The Seduction, Heaven
and Hell* is clearly a much more important play. In it all of
Kornfeld's Expressionist ideas and experiments reach their full
fruition, however problematical the outcome may be in the final
analysis. Although he was probably working on the play during
1916–17, a complete version did not appear in print until after
the end of hostilities in 1919. An important sequence from it
had, however, appeared already in Przygode's *Die Dichtung* in
the autumn of 1918. The première took place in Reinhardt's
Deutsches Theater on April 21, 1920, under the direction of
Ludwig Berger, who was able to discuss the production with
Kornfeld beforehand, and so to gain the author's approval of
his interpretation.[13] Leading critics like Julius Bab and Siegfried
Jacobson praised the production and acclaimed the literary value
of the text; the public, however, was not impressed, and the
play was taken off after only two nights. Since then it has survived only in histories of literature and of the theater.

The most important element to emerge from a study of the
text is its religiosity. Despite the excess of bizarre crimes and
apparent delight in sexual perversities (e.g., the lesbian relationship between Johanna and Maria, and the purely sexual relationship between Leonhard and the countess), this is indeed the
aim of the play. The names of the principal characters already
indicate this fact: Esther, Maria, Jakob, and Johanna are all
taken from the biblical sphere, while Beate is short for Beatrix,
the name of a saint. More specifically, the language of the play
immediately strikes the religious note with its echoes of Klop-
stock and the Old Testament, while the climax, showing the
ascent of the souls to heavenly salvation, is the final proof of

the religious aim of the play. Not that religion can here be
defined in any narrowly dogmatic sense; what the play demonstrates is rather a religious awareness, a quest for religious
values, however disruptive of traditional beliefs this may be.
Hence Kornfeld is not an exponent of "bad Catholicism"; he is
groping toward a new form of mystery play from within the
Old Testament-Jewish sphere, but yet with great stress on
suffering saints and miracles.

The roots of Kornfeld's thinking are not difficult to find.
There are, for example, many obvious echoes of Goethe's *Faust*,
not only in the language, but also in the theme of "Das Ewig-
Weibliche." But more important than Goethe, whom Kornfeld
almost literally worshipped, are the traces of Dostoyevsky and
Strindberg. From Dostoyevsky Kornfeld took the "ecstatic hell
of the soul," and from Strindberg, the theme of marriage as
hell on earth, showing people without love chained together in
hatred and misunderstanding, while filled with the eternal longing for salvation and for an end to suffering. This is the theme
of Kornfeld's play: the release of men and women from a
"hellish" existence of suffering and misfortune, into a "heavenly"
supraterrestrial reality. Salvation comes as an act of grace, when
the three women reach the ultimate in suffering and thereby
release the soul of one man. As in *The Seduction*, the primacy
of the soul is what must be demonstrated, but whereas *The
Seduction* verged on nihilism in its despair at the world, *Heaven
and Hell* does arrive at a more balanced view, accepting both
heaven and hell, good and evil, happiness and unhappiness.

The means whereby Kornfeld imparts this view are developed
from the techniques employed in *The Seduction*. The plot is
deliberately trivial; logical and causal connections are treated
in an incredibly cavalier fashion; and there is absolutely no
attempt at natural psychology or *vraisemblance*. So, for example,
Maria tells the story of her baby and how she threw it into
the water, because it would have starved to death anyway, and
how she then watched the pike shoot up and pull the little
bundle down into the depths. "On the basis of facts and proof"
Maria is falsely accused of murdering the countess; Johanna
is pardoned by the judges at first, although she has committed a
murder; Maria is not pardoned although she is innocent; Maria

and Johanna, the prostitutes, are treated as positive figures, while "respectable" characters like the countess and the marchioness are clearly negative. The ones who go to heaven are characters like Beate and Johanna who have killed and committed real crimes, while those who have lived blameless lives are consigned to hell.

Kornfeld has clearly written a Wandlungsdrama: at the beginning the count and Beate are living in a soulless state of lethargy of the heart. The introduction of the prostitute into their household sets everybody into chaotic motion, yet out of this chaos something fruitful does emerge. One indication that Kornfeld's position has moved from the almost totally tragic vision of *The Seduction* is, as has been noted, the ending, which is now in heaven instead of being under the sign of demons and chaos, as in the earlier work; but another indication is the alternation of verse and prose in *Heaven and Hell*. This imparts an ethereal quality to the whole work, as against the earth-bound character of *The Seduction*. The same applies to the general structure of the play. Where *The Seduction* was based, like many early Expressionistic works, on a solipsistic monologue form, focused on the single protagonist, *Heaven and Hell* has developed into a complex arrangement of dialogues, although long monologues are not entirely banished. As in *The Seduction*, the result is high pathos in the Expressionist manner, hymnic utterance—opera!

The emphasis on opera more than anything is the source of Kornfeld's failure. The visual element of drama is almost totally eliminated, and his theater is reduced to a symphony of voices, all proclaiming the need to transcend the world. There is simply nothing left for the audience except the tension between absolute good and absolute evil—evil being life on this earth, while good is the heavenly paradise. And as this is a polarity which goes beyond the human level into the abstract, all the characters dissolve into transparent embodiments of abstract concepts.

Kornfeld was by no means alone in his attempt to create a modern mystery play. Csokor's *Der grosse Kampf* (The Great Struggle [1914]), Becker's *Das letzte Gericht* (The Last Judgment [1919]), Dietzenschmidt's *Christofer* (1920), and even Kaiser's *Hölle Weg Erde* (Hell Way Earth [1919]) all point in

the same direction; but Kornfeld was certainly the most consistent in his spiritual endeavors, both in theory and in practice,
and his failure, if it was one, was on a grand scale.

## V  *Franz Werfel*

Another product of the German-Jewish circle in Prague was
Franz Werfel (1890–1945).[14] Like Kornfeld, he adopted at an
early stage an extreme religious, antipolitical stance. Kornfeld
became famous for his metapolitics, rejecting all involvement
by the artist in party political issues and day-to-day affairs of
government. Werfel made his views known in his essay, "Die
Christliche Sendung" (The Christian Mission), which appeared
in the January, 1917, number of *Die neue Rundschau*.[15] Although,
as will be seen, Werfel was by this time involved in a considerable public controversy, he had originally made his name as a
poet, not as a religious propagandist—indeed, his volume of
poems, *Der Weltfreund* (Friend to Mankind), published in
Berlin in 1911 by Axel Juncker (Rilke's first publisher), was one
of *the* literary sensations of the Expressionist generation.

In the autumn of 1912 Werfel left Prague for Leipzig, where
he became a reader with the newly established publishing house
of Kurt Wolff, a name associated with the first appearance in
print of so many Expressionists. While with Kurt Wolff from
1912 until 1914, Werfel's lyrical vein remained remarkably fruitful, and he completed *Wir Sind* (We Are [1913]) and *Einander*
(One Another [1915]).

Although he first made his name as a poet, Werfel had from
a very early stage been interested in drama. His *Der Besuch aus
dem Elysium* (Visit from Elysium [1912]), a lyrical drama, did
not, unfortunately, achieve the same success as *Friend to Mankind*, although it was written about this time; and the same was
true of *Die Versuchung. Ein Gespräch des Dichters mit dem
Erzengel und Luzifer* (Temptation, a Conversation Between the
Poet, the Archangel and Lucifer [1913]), which, despite its lack
of theatrical success, is still interesting as an early expression
of the poet's exclusive devotion to his mission and his complete
rejection of any desire to reshape society or reform the world.
The "temptation" of the title is modeled on the temptation of
Christ, and the Devil is closely identified with political power:

I'll fill you so full with disgust and pity, that you'll roar over parliaments, congresses and world gatherings like a Samum. I'll make you so mad at what you encounter that you'll be capable of unheard-of courage and unheard-of deeds. You shall feel bliss! One against millions. And you shall die the death of deaths. In triumph, in victory, either at the hands of a bomb-thrower or by a bullet from a helpless enemy after the earthquake of one of your speeches.[16]

As with Kornfeld, Werfel's theme is, in effect, the struggle between good and evil, only here the ideal goal is that form of universal kinship suggested by the poems of *Friend to Mankind.*

Much more effective as a play was Werfel's adaptation of Euripides' *Die Troerinnen* (The Trojan Women), published in 1915.[17] Although he stayed very close to the original, the very fact that he had chosen this particular text was thought significant; indeed, it was assumed that the antiwar stance of the play was a result of Werfel's own feelings about the war itself; he was from the outset an outspoken pacifist. However, he had already completed his translation before the start of the First World War. This version, appearing as it did in 1915, and being performed in April, 1916, in the Lessing Theater in Berlin, was a theatrical event of considerable magnitude. The theme of the play was explosive enough without the context of the actual war, and Werfel's treatment pointed up the modernity and relevance of it all.

As in so many Expressionist plays of classical form there was little or no plot as such, but plenty of scope for screams, madness, ecstasy, and wild accusation, expressed in lyrical-rhetorical language. For this generation of Germans the antimilitarist meaning of the adaptation seemed clear. After the war Werfel felt compelled to carry out considerable revisions which muted the pacifist power of his first version and moved the whole further away from the Greek original toward his own ideal of Christianity and humanity. Werfel had earlier become involved in a dispute with activists like Kurt Hiller over his religious interpretation of *The Trojan Women*; and indeed it was this dispute with Kurt Hiller that had given rise to his open letter entitled "The Christian Mission" in which he publicly renounced political action as a solution to the world's problems and proclaimed his faith in Christianity. Replies to Werfel's open letter were not slow in coming, particularly from Jewish writers like Max Brod and philosophers of religion like Gustav Landauer. The most bitter outcome of the public debate was the resulting split between Werfel and Karl Kraus, who, from being one of his earliest admirers, became one of his most unrelenting foes. This feud was to come to a head over Werfel's most significant play of the Expressionist period, *Spiegelmensch* (Mirror Man).

Werfel was by this time a public figure, famous not only for his poetry but also for his magnificent reading voice. Despite his opposition to the war and his denunciation of it in poems and other literary works, he served in the Austrian army and in accordance with the Austrian tradition of safeguarding poets was eventually found a safe posting to the Press Section along with Rilke, Hofmannsthal, Musil, and other writers. It was through one of his literary associates here, Franz Blei, that he met his future wife, the lovely intellectual, Alma, widow of the composer Gustav Mahler and at that time still the wife of the famous architect, Walter Gropius. Right up to the end of the war, Werfel continued his pacifist writings and activities and, on the collapse following the end of the hostilities, even became involved for a time in the revolutionary aftermath. But economic issues and class warfare were clearly not for him, and he soon returned to his basic religious messianism.

The postwar years in Vienna found Werfel still writing in an Expressionistic vein, especially in a prose narrative work like *Nicht der Mörder, der Ermordete ist schuldig* (The Victim Not the Murderer is the Guilty One [1920]) which takes up the father-son conflict within a political framework of patriarchal power. But it is interesting that Werfel also continued writing for the theater with *Die Mittagsgöttin, Spiegelmensch, Bocksgesang*, and *Schweiger*. *Die Mittagsgöttin* (Noon Goddess [1919]) deals with yet another of the quintessential themes of the age of Expressionism, the idea of regression. The possibility which Werfel conjures up in this *Zauberspiel* is that of leaving the complications of the modern world behind and going back to a less complicated state, to a kind of Golden Age.

*Bocksgesang* (Goat Song [1912]) is Werfel's first drama in prose. The title is a literal translation of the Greek "tragedia" and means not only tragedy, but also the song of the goat, which was sung during the rites of Dionysios. When it was first performed in the Raimund Theater in Vienna in March, 1922, the public and the critics found the play revolutionary, confusing, and incomprehensible, though there was no doubting the lyrical intensity and poetic beauty of the language. Since then, appreciation of the dramatic power, the mythical background and the grotesque treatment of certain parts has grown, and the prophetic quality of the play has been singled out for particular praise for its early awareness of the ineradicable presence of evil in the world. With specific reference to Hitler and National Socialism it has been said: "After experiencing our recent past, it may not be at all impossible for us to imagine a 'Beast,' enshrined and worshipped with outstretched hands and frenzied cries, demanding its innumerable human victims and laying waste to an entire continent."[18] *Goat Song* was performed by the Theater Guild in New York on January 25, 1926, in Ruth Langer's translation, with Alfred Lunt, Lynn Fontaine, and Blanche Murka in the leading roles. It was a financial success, not least because of the colorful costumes and attractive stage designs by Lee Simonson. All in all it was acclaimed as the event of the theatrical season, causing Eugene O'Neill to describe it "as a play which really justifies all one can say by way of enthusiastic praise."

Werfel's last play of his Expressionist period, *Schweiger* (1922), was not welcomed with such "enthusiastic praise"; indeed, from its first appearance it received an extremely mixed critical reception, though it proved popular with theater audiences, both in German-speaking countries and abroad. Through the figure of Schweiger (in his notes Werfel had first called him not Schweiger, i.e., The Taciturn One, but "Mass-Murderer") Werfel wanted to crystallize various forces, which, like the forces of evil in *Goat Song*, he felt to be in the air at the time—socialism, the lust for power, psychotic drives, etc. All of these are shown tearing at the soul of poor Schweiger. Such complex motivation did not make for clarity of plot or intention, and the play was condemned for its mixture of "politics, psychiatry and mysticism," and accused of being an "impossible conglomeration of psychic and physical abnormalities." Kafka in particular, whom Werfel, as a fellow Prague writer, knew well, felt compelled to reject the play outright because he thought that Werfel had trivialized the basic dilemma of his generation by reducing it to the mental imbalance of one particular individual (though the real reason for his objection was probably the psychiatric content).[19]

But however powerful a play like *Schweiger* might be, and however intense the author in his quest for redemption, there is no doubting the preeminence of Werfel's earlier play, *Mirror Man* (1920), as the closest he came during his Expressionist period to creating a masterpiece. This magic trilogy was published by the Kurt Wolff Verlag in 1920 and received its première on October 15, 1921, in Leipzig and Stuttgart.[20] As a trilogy it is already far wider in scope than *The Noon Goddess, Goat Song,* or *Schweiger.* This scope is expanded even further by making it a magic trilogy, for magic has the power to fuse the otherwise disparate worlds of dream and reality, subject and object, appearance, and essence. It is consonant, too, with this magic goal that Werfel should portray his two main characters not as individuals or types but as allegorical figures. The dramatic heart of the play is the Faustian motif of the "*two* souls within the human breast," the second of which is brought to life by the magic of the mirror.

The play itself has no plot as such, but instead a revue structure familiar from Goethe's *Faust II* and Ibsen's *Peer Gynt,* which allows the protagonist to be exposed to the whole of life with all its temptations. The setting for the first part is a magically remote place in a legendary highland, that of the second part a "phantastic Orient," while the end of the play opens up into a panoramic view through a mirror-window into a higher reality. The play thereby moves *out* into the world, while at the same time creating the impression that everything is contained *within* the poetic imagination of the single protagonist. The main impression is of a bewildering series of images proceeding from the vast emptiness of the initial mountain landscape and the monastery to the father's house, the palace terrace, the temple yard in Chilshamba, the prison, the courtroom, and so on. By constantly changing scenery and by the use of lighting Werfel hoped to create the atmosphere of a magically remote unreal world, an aim reinforced in practice on the stage (as it turned out) by the use of back-projection and filmed material.

But the main way in which Werfel expressed the superficiality of the "real" world was through constant movement. Spiegelmensch, the Mirror-Man, is characterized by mad dancing, leaping, climbing, and tumbling; and Fissilih, the dancing girl, also twirls and spins. Truth and purity, by contrast, are motionless, as in the unchanging ritual and static poses of the monks in the monastery. This choreographic element is absolutely fundamental to the structure of the play; indeed, Werfel had originally planned it as a mime-ballet to be worked out between man and mirror-man. Even in the final version there is still one totally wordless scene in which the double mimes the act of love. The combination of static and dynamic, stillness and movement are basic to the nature of Expressionism, but in this play Werfel has extended this technique to embrace an allegorical dimension. Movement predominates in the play, reflecting the path of man through a false reality, before he at last penetrates to the stillness of truth and purity.

In Werfel's early works, language was linked with music by its lyrical character. In *Mirror Man*, too, Werfel's language shows musical elements through its rich rhymes and rhythms. Sometimes indeed the richness goes too far and the lines become empty jingles, of a kind associated with operatic libretti rather than serious drama. In addition, on numerous occasions instrumental music takes over from the dialogue, and there are marches with drums, gongs, and little bells; ecstatic scenes with trumpets and bagpipes; and yet other scenes filled with hunting horns, whistles, and animal sounds. All this is operatic theatricality developed to an extremely high level; yet the scenic and acoustic riches are not there for their own sake—they are intended rather to overwhelm the audience with the magic of the stage. As Werfel himself put it: "This is a colossus, but hugely theatrical: tragedy, farce, opera, ballet and allegory all rolled into one. I don't know whether I am a dramatist, but I do know that there is nobody writing today who has as much theater in him as I have."[21]

In part, what he is attempting in *Mirror Man* is consonant with the general movement toward theatricality in Expressionism;

but this is only part of the explanation, because Werfel's aims go beyond mere entertainment. He clearly intends to transport each member of the audience out of himself into another world, making the theater into a magic place, which has its own power over him, freeing him, as a heathen cult, from the tensions of the real world. This basic idea of a quasi-dionysiac theatrical cult-ceremony is further developed into the goal of salvation through the esthetic experience. Just as Thamal in the play loses himself in order to find himself, so too each member of the audience must lose himself and learn to reject the false temptations of a real world, which is presented as incapable of change by any action on his part. Little wonder that Brecht, who believed in clear-minded rationality and the need to change the world, totally rejected Werfel's quietism.

On the whole, although the première of *Mirror Man* in October, 1921, was a resounding success and Werfel, who was present in Leipzig, was repeatedly called to take a bow with the producer, Dr. Alwin Kronacher, the play found lasting success neither with the critics nor with the public.[22] For a start, the parallels with the masterpieces of other ages and other countries were too oppressively omnipresent. *Mirror Man* was compared with Wolfram's *Parzival*, Goethe's *Faust*, Ibsen's *Peer Gynt*, Hofmannsthal's *Everyman*, Schikaneder's *Magic Flute*, Calderón's *La Vida es sueño*, Grillparzer's *Der Traum ein Leben* (The Dream a Life), and Strindberg's *To Damascus*, not to mention Raimund's popular magic theater. It proved too easy to dismiss *Mirror Man* as derivative and merely imitative.

Further, the play was extremely difficult to stage, and its multiplicity of scene changes put it outside the scope of all theaters except those with the fullest range of professional actors and stage machinery. Nor had Werfel made it easy for himself by using the contemporary references with which he laced his text. As a result, both the Nationalists and the followers of Karl Kraus were deeply offended by certain passages and threatened a theater scandal on the occasion of the Austrian première in Vienna in 1922. For security reasons the performance took place under police protection. In the event cuts to the text had removed the offending passages (and much of the sense of the play as well), and the threatened scandal did not take place.

Ancient literary feuds are rarely of lasting interest, and that between Karl Kraus and Werfel has not much to redeem it; nevertheless, one must face up to the question of who was right.[23] Had Werfel created a masterpiece replete with religious wisdom and prophetic insight into the dangers of the Führer mentality; or was he, as Karl Kraus suggested, merely a benevolent windbag with a talent for letting off metaphysical steam? Time has told against Werfel, and while one can understand the success of the various productions of *Mirror Man* around the German-speaking world in the 1920's, the magic has faded as the century has proceeded, and the mixture of Babylonian myth, Indian mysticism, Buddhist faith, and Christian renunciation tends to be more than the modern literary palate can stand.

## V  *Carl Einstein*

Two of the writers considered so far in this chapter on the religious drama of German Expressionism were Jewish, and, as has been seen in the controversy between Kurt Hiller, Max Brod, Karl Kraus, and Franz Werfel over the latter's "Christian Mission," there was almost bound to be trouble as a result. The same was the case with Carl Einstein (1885–1940) who became involved in one of the great *causes célèbres* of the age through his blasphemy trial. Einstein, the son of a famous Jewish rabbi, grew up and went to school in Karlsruhe, which he left at the age of nineteen for Berlin. He quickly became one of the leading literary figures of that extraordinary city and a great authority on modern and African art with a wide range of acquaintances that included all the leading figures in the European art world of that time. He contributed to Franz Blei's *Hyperion*, to Pfemfert's *Die Aktion*, and edited the satirical journal, *Der blutige Ernst* (Deadly Earnest), with George Grosz. He was friendly with André Gide, Mayakovsky, and Meyerhold and was an editor of Eugene Jolas' *transition*, the journal which published sections from his experiment in absolute prose, the novel *Bebuquin*, alongside James Joyce's "Work in Progress."[24]

During the war years Einstein was, with interruptions, a soldier, and, in the disturbances that followed, he fought on the side of the Spartacists in Berlin (1918/19), though he would

never have allowed himself to be described as a doctrinaire
Communist Party member. He was a freedom-fighter then, just
as he was later when he followed the call to fight in Spain
against Franco. In 1940 he was interned, as were all Germans
living in France, and sent to the south of France. As a former
soldier on the side of the Spanish republicans there was no
possibility of escape for him with the others who went over
the Pyrenees into Spain: capture by the approaching Germans
meant death as a Jew, and so on July 5, 1940, he decided
to commit suicide, slashed his wrists, and threw himself into
the Gave de Pau.

What we are concerned with here is not Einstein, the art
historian, though his work on African sculpture exercised enormous influence at this time; not Einstein, the exponent of
experimental prose or avant-garde intellectual poetry; but Einstein, the dramatist. In this connection it is worth spending a
little time on his mime, *Nuronihar*, first published in *Die Aktion*
in 1914, not least because of its parallels with Werfel's *Mirror
Man* in particular, and the Expressionist generation's fascination
with the art of the dance in general.[25]

The subject matter of the piece seems to be taken from William
Beckford's *Vathek*, which Einstein admired. But more interesting
than the exotic-oriental background is the way in which setting
and dance are described. Everything must be "un-naturalistic";
there must be no trace of psychology; classical dance, full of
pirouettes, pas and pointes, is dismissed as "sweet" and "silly,"
while Nuronihar is projected as *the* dancer because her dancing
is total, embracing her whole being. The story, such as it is,
is simple: Vathek, the godlike tyrant, is finally overcome by
the tiny dancing girl. The last of the three scenes takes place
in Vathek's tent, although the stage is completely filled with
the cathedral-like palace of Eblis. After an extremely erotic
sequence in which Nuronihar casts off her veils, she slays Vathek
with his own sword, enters the temple and dies in a pillar of
light, suffering the most extreme of tortures in the ecstasy of
her last exotic dance.

It was not this combination of religion and ecstasy which
attracted the attention of the state's moral mentors, but the
dramatic sequence in twenty scenes called *Die schlimme Bot-*

*schaft* (The Terrible Message) which Einstein published in Berlin in 1921. What he did was to imagine what would happen if Jesus were alive in the third year of the new republic of Germany. Jesus is presented as a very mild Communist-idealist who is ill-treated, abused, and finally killed by the degenerate specimens of humanity he encounters. The very first scene, *Jesus und der Bürger* (Jesus and the member of the middle class), immediately makes clear what He has to expect in the modern world, for He is accused of sticking His nose into matters which are no concern of His and stirring up the poor to protest. The next scenes follow the traditional stages of the story of the passion of Christ. It is perhaps in the last sequence of scenes that Einstein has most satirical fun, when he shows Jesus being talked about by magistrates (a common target in Germany in an age of reactionary class-biased hanging-judges), and by businessmen, Jews, Nationalists, esthetes, and art dealers. Einstein even has the crucifixion story taken over by the world of the cinema and is not above making a few digs at the exaggerations of the Expressionist style itself:

FILM STAR PISSY PUCK: You can see how unsatisfactory Naturalism is. The fellow looks ridiculously wretched, like any old common criminal.

FILM DIRECTOR: Maybe, but that doesn't mean going overboard for Expressionism.

PISSY PUCK: This is what the face should look like. (*Bares her teeth and rolls her fiery eyes.*)[26]

In a later scene, Einstein, who, as an art critic himself, was well aware of the Expressionists' love of Grünewald-type depictions of the crucifixion, has an art dealer sitting in his car under the cross, engaged in a discussion of the crucifixion as an art theme with Pissy Puck, who this time advises the mother of Christ on the most suitable facial expression:

PISSY PUCK: Actually the whole theme is Expressionistic. All the same Mary is not showing that properly. (*To Mary*) Dear Lady, you ought to do this. More despair, more despair! More of the Negro!

LITTLE DEALER: More of the nigger![27]

Before the end, Jesus on the cross has been described again as "Expressionistic," "gothic," "cosmic," and a whole Expressionist painting class has arrived to practice depicting the scene.

It is clear that Einstein, despite his serious intention, was also having a great deal of fun with the story of Jesus on the cross. This was not, however, how the reviewers of the provincial newspapers in Germany took it. These backwoodsmen simply thought of Einstein, the Jew, being offensive at the expense of the Christian religion. In support of this contention four quotations from the text were printed completely out of context, whereupon the powerful and reactionary *Kreuzzeitung* picked up the story and printed the quotations. A businessman from Reutlingen read these and himself published a notice inviting any others who had been as disgusted as he had to write in, so that a case could be brought against the offending work. He received two replies in all, but still made a case of it. He had not at this point read the book itself. The public prosecutor's office agreed to pursue the matter. The court proceedings which followed would have been judged ludicrously funny if they had not at the same time cast an extremely revealing light on the reactionary nature of German justice in the republic.

Speaking on his behalf Einstein had a body of serious intellectuals and artists, including Käthe Kollwitz. They were hardly listened to by the court. Speaking against, as expert witnesses on religion, were authorities like the Reverend Mauff from the Kaiser-Wilhelm-Gedächtnis-Kirche, who told the court that he felt compelled to reject this work by Einstein because it was "Expressionistic." When asked by counsel what he meant he became red in the face and screamed with rage: "By Expressionism I mean treating with contempt, ridiculing and casting in the dust everything that is lofty and worthwhile; Expressionism is the art of Bolshevists and Anarchists!"[28] When asked how he knew this he admitted that he had never seen an Expressionistic work in his life; he had read this in a certain history of literature. Worse than this was the behavior of the public prosecutor who was quite openly anti-Semitic. He began his summing-up with the words: "the accused, Einstein, is a Jew. A Jew has no religious confession and is therefore by definition areligious." Carl Einstein was condemned to six weeks' imprisonment and his publisher to three weeks, sentences commuted to fines of 10,000 and 5,000 marks, respectively.

## VI  *Ernst Barlach*

One of the features of the Expressionist religious drama is that it deals with seeking, as distinct from finding or knowing, God. In this connection, Ernst Barlach (1870–1938) seems the God-seeker par excellence. There is perhaps no need to deal with him in depth here, for one thing because his work is often considered peripheral to the Expressionist movement as such, and for another because a separate volume in this series has already been devoted to his dramatic works. Nevertheless, there is no doubting the power and importance of his religious dramas, the most important of which enjoyed significant productions by leading producers of the age.

The mark of a Barlach play, apart from the tortured unnatural language, is the extremely accurate picture he conjures up of small-town life in North Germany. But despite this, Barlach is far removed from any naturalistic intention of portraying social or economic conditions or advocating any kind of reform. What he seems to demonstrate is yet again that man is not determined by milieu, race, class, or any other such conditioning factor. Man is neither a machine nor a mere animal predestined to travel along certain paths. He is free to choose his own path. Put another way, this makes his plays revolve around the fundamental Expressionist theme of the regeneration of man, the birth of the New Man. Always in Barlach there are concrete images to express this abstract meaning, yet at the same time his plays remain *Entscheidungsdramen*, plays involving some fundamental decision; and they remain clearly in the tradition of the play of ideas, with the result that the intellectual content often makes his plays rather dense, especially as the message, such as it is, is expressed not in language of sustained pathos, but in an awkward, earthy, groping style, which, like the theme of his plays, also seems to be in a state of becoming. Characteristically, too, his plays are full of grotesque characters, incidents, and situations, which also avoid the dangers of excessive elevation of tone. But the striking feature is still that fundamental to all Expressionist drama, namely, the *vision*. Even in the normal life of simple people in a small town in North Germany the world of values behind the world of appearances can suddenly be revealed. Eyes are opened to *see*!

Barlach was not only a great sculptor; he was also a great literary artist. The Expressionist movement from Kokoschka on was characterized (as has been seen) by constant cross-fertilization among the arts from painting and sculpture to music and mime, but Barlach was perhaps the only one of the artists to create major work in the literary as well as the artistic field. His plays are among the most significant achievements of modern German drama.

## VII  *Hans Henny Jahnn*

The next writer to be considered, Hans Henny Jahnn (1894–1959), was a North German God-seeker like Barlach, with whom he has often been compared; and like Barlach he made his name in another art outside literature, this time music, not painting or sculpture. Born in the Hamburg suburb of Stellingen he was already writing dramas in school, but when he left he became an organ-builder. In the course of his life he rediscovered the secrets of the Baroque organ and saved and restored many instruments. As a result he was in a position to reform the whole art of European organ-building. In addition, he organized, at great personal sacrifice, complete critical editions of Baroque musicians like Arnold Schlick, Vincent Lübeck, Samuel Scheidt, and Dietrich Buxtehude. Next to music his great love was architecture.

His life was not an easy one. He went into exile twice, once to Norway in 1915, when he was twenty, and yet again in 1933 when he was thirty-nine. The Nazis banned his plays *Strassenecke* (Street Corner) and *Neuer Lübecker Totentanz* (New Lübeck Dance of Death), and he made his way through Switzerland to Denmark, where he purchased a farm on Bornholm, bred horses, and engaged in hormone research. The love of horses is a recurring theme in his work. Each time he returned to Germany once the war was over, in 1918 and 1945. He was an out-and-out pacifist, against any kind of violence, against war, race hatred, the death penalty, or the slaughtering of animals.

As far as Jahnn's dramas are concerned, it was rather difficult to form any clear picture of their worth until Walter Muschg published a collection of them in 1963. As he put it, "they were an essential component of the Expressionist theater, but on the stage they only managed a problematical existence, were shrouded in scandal, and essentially belong to the genre of the visionary fantasy drama, which possesses such a lofty tradition in German."[29] The massive book was at first sold only to those who were over eighteen years, were prepared to declare that they were purchasing it exclusively for their own private use and would not give or lend the book to minors. Jahnn was clearly a fanatical writer—Muschg reports finding twenty-two manuscripts of dramatic works written before *Pastor Ephraim Magnus* (1919), his first published play.[30] These are, on the whole, turn-of-the-century exercises in Neo-Romanticism and in the poetry of puberty; nevertheless, one or two of the titles are pointers to later developments in Expressionism (for example, *Revolution* and *Jesus Christ*), and one of his later plays, *Heinrich von Kleist*, was published in an almanac edited by Carl Einstein. Of his plays written in the Expressionist manner *Die Krönung Richards III* (The Coronation of Richard III) enjoyed a reasonably successful run in the Schauspielhaus, Leipzig, in 1922, and has been reissued recently,[31] while his *Medea* (with Agnes Straub as a Negress Medea) also enjoyed a sensational première in the Staatliches Schauspielhaus, Berlin, under the direction of Jürgen Fehling. It has been reprinted and performed again since then in the sixties.[32]

To gain some idea of the essence of Jahnn's work it is perhaps advisable to concentrate here specifically on his first and most sensational published work, *Pastor Ephraim Magnus*, the "award-winning drama of an erotomaniac."[33] This phrase was the title given by Edgar Gross to his review of the play in *Das literarische Echo*. The award he refers to was the prestigious Kleist prize, bestowed upon the play by the judge for that year, Oskar Loerke, who was quickly called upon from various quarters to defend his choice. One reason for the selection is, however, obvious: Kleist is referred to on the publishers' dust-cover to the play, and the parallels with Kleist's strangely distorted, unnatural syntax, and the equally unnatural sexuality of Kleist's

*Penthesilea* readily spring to mind. The author himself refers to *Woyzeck* and the Marquis de Sade, while Gross detected echoes of Grabbe's *Gothland*, as well as of other less likely literary predecessors, like Zacharias Werner (for necrophilia). Gross is clearly not favorably impressed by this work in which he sees nothing but the "infinite wallowing in perversity of a sick mind," nor is the subject matter elevated, as far as he is concerned, by any stylistic or formal felicities; on the contrary, Jahnn seems to Gross a mere beginner, lost in unproductive formlessness, stringing together images in epic arbitrariness without any regard for form, and stumbling from one vast monologue on the mysteries of the human soul to another. Another contemporary review, this time by H. Pankow, while accepting the idea that Jahnn is a God-seeker, nevertheless sees in the work, "some approaches to drama only as far as form is concerned, otherwise in content the product of an apparently extremely meagre, but at the same time fundamentally sick, sexually perverted imagination, full of unspeakable filth."[34]

Perhaps the fairest contemporary assessment of Jahnn's play is that by the famous drama critic, Julius Bab.[35] He at least realized that Loerke was a literary judge who had to be taken seriously, and so he spent months over Jahnn's text, months filled with pain and horror at what he was reading, which is why he could only read a few paragraphs at a time, and yet by the end he was prepared to admit that it had been worth the effort. Jahnn was not, in his view, a true dramatist, despite the Storm and Stress style, because he failed to create separate individuals who came to life. Instead, Bab saw Jahnn essentially as a philosophical, religious writer employing dialogue form, while the tragic problem Jahnn was dealing with (as he saw it) was the independent existence of the body. Jahnn refuses to ignore the body: instead he focuses attention on it in his attempt to get beyond it to the spirit. This is why there is such stress on every possible physical function, especially sexual, with such utter brutality. The possibilities of every organ must be absolutely exhausted. As Bab sees it, this work represents the absolute limit, which is its cultural-historical significance: "An extreme point is reached. And thus the book acquires a meaning for everyone who wants to find his bearings in the intellectual climate of the age."

A glance at the *dramatis personae* reveals that the play contains many of the standard ingredients of Expressionist drama, first of all father and son (Pastor Magnus and the son Ephraim of the title), although the Pastor also has an illegitimate son, Jakob. The main burden of the plot is carried by Ephraim and Jakob, the two sons, together with Johanna the daughter. Jakob becomes a sex-murderer (another favorite motif of Expressionist dramatic art from Wedekind's Jack-the-Ripper onward), and as a result, there is also an extensive courtroom scene in the play with the traditional representatives of bourgeois justice. That the level of action is not restricted to the merely real is indicated by the Dance of Death of the four apparitions who appear to Ephraim and Johanna, namely, a Beheaded, a Crucified, a Castrated, and a Handless Man. Jahnn had a particular predilection for boys (though not in any homosexual sense), and there are various young men in the *dramatis personae*, including the two who indulge in fellatio, in the scene at which Edgar Gross took particular offense: ". . . this drama should be pulped immediately. The only future it can possibly have is for one rare copy to be preserved in a collection of pornographic exotica. The scene in which two boys practice sexual aberrations on each other shows this quite clearly."[36]

The play starts as a "scream play," with the father longing for death and release from the burden of the flesh. Jakob, the illegitimate son, leaves him a gun. This initial scene with the father represents the point of departure from which the three God-seekers—Ephraim, Jakob, and Johanna—will set out on their quest. It also offers some clue both to the nature of Jahnn's style and to the mystery he is striving for. Firstly, why is Jahnn's play so inordinately long? The Pastor's own words give some answer: "because every word spoken needs a hundred words of explanation, because it is so difficult to say the simple things." Once, Pastor Magnus claims, it was possible to *live* the simple things, but this has been lost in the modern age. So, like Gottfried Benn, Kornfeld, and others, Jahnn is urging a form of regression to a mythic, primeval state. That is why the world he conjures up in his floods of words is so chaotic and barbaric.

The father, before he dies, proclaims two possible paths through
life apart from the path of death he takes himself:

Es gibt nur zwei Wege, die Sicherheit bergen. Der eine ist köstlich,
der andere furchtbar. Der eine ist: die Dinge leben, die gewollt sind,
ganz restlos ohne Rücksicht—lieben, Liebe leisten, so wie Gott es
wollte: freveln. Und der andere: Gott gleich werden, alle Qualen
auf sich nehmen, ohne je erlöst zu werden; denn so ist Gott, nachdem
man seine Liebe verschmähte und ihn ans Kreuz schlug. Es ist nur
die Dunkelheit der Nöte in ihm.—Und was ihr grausames jemandem
tut, das tut ihr Gott.

(There are only two paths which promise certainty. One is delight-
ful, the other terrible. One is to live the things wanted, out and
out, regardless—to love, offer love, as God wanted: to sin. And the
other is to become as God, take all sufferings upon oneself without
finding salvation; for this is how God is, since his love was rejected
and he was nailed to the cross. There is only the darkness of sufferings
in him—And whatever cruelty you inflict on anyone you inflict
on God.)

These two paths are then followed by his children. The
illegitimate son, Jakob, follows the path of love and the flesh
and ends up slaughtering a woman and ripping the body apart
in his quest for the soul. His brother, Ephraim, who has accepted
the Establishment position of cathedral preacher, follows the
alternative path of suffering. He has himself tortured and crucified by his sister Johanna, and by the end he is mutilated,
castrated, and blind. His relationship with Johanna has, in the
meantime, been strangely incestuous, and when she dies he
places her body with that of his brother Jakob in the same
coffin. The decay of the dead flesh which he dreads is halted;
a miracle takes place, and the two become marble statues. The
end of the play sees Magnus adored as a saint and working
as a master-builder on a memorial chapel to be added to
the cathedral.

This very brief and very approximate account of the "plot"
can take no account of the vast monologues and the welter of
gruesome details; and the wonder is that such a play should
have been performed at all. Yet performed it was in Berlin in

August, 1923, in a private club called Das Theater organized by Dr. Jo Lhermann. Arnolt Bronnen, who had been looking for something sensational with which to open this theater, remembered Jahnn's mystery play. He was also attracted by the similarities between himself and Jahnn: "Like Bronnen, Jahnn wanted an analysis of the flesh, a science of emotion, an algebra of nerves. While Bronnen employed erotic orgies as means of analysis, Jahnn dissected the powerfully thundering organ of human passion, with all the means of torture, cruelty and bestiality going straight to the absolute limits."[37] While Bronnen looked after the production side, Brecht agreed to prune the text for performance, which meant cutting the three hundred pages of text (taking perhaps some seven hours of acting time) down to two hours. The result was not a success in the eyes of either the author or the public, and the theatrical venture was closed by the police after one week.

## VIII  *Alfred Brust*

Another forgotten God-seeker of the Expressionist generation who has recently been rediscovered, not least for his similarities with the contemporary Jesus cult and the hippie-commune movement is Alfred Brust (1891–1934).[38] Brust was born in the far northeast of Germany, in East Prussia, and, like Barlach, was to look further east to Russia as the land of true soul and simplicity. Like Jahnn, he discovered Kleist at an early age and also shared the Nietzsche enthusiasm of this generation. After having been proposed many times for the coveted Kleist Prize, he won it at last in 1929. Brust wrote many plays and as a Kurt Wolff author was looked upon as one of the most promising dramatists of the time; yet despite many performances and some discussion of his work, for the greater part of his life he lived cut off from the mainstream, complaining of lack of recognition.

Now, with hindsight, it can be seen that he was in many ways a peculiarly representative figure. That he was a God-seeker the very titles of his plays reveal: e.g., *Der ewige Mensch, Drama in Christo* (Eternal Man, Drama in Christ [1919]) and *Die Schlacht der Heilande* (The Battle of the Saviors [1920]). He also shared the taste of the age for the exotic East and the South Seas and set some of his plays accordingly, for example, *Das indische Spiel* (The Indian Play). With Jahnn he also shared the taste for the theater of cruelty and the idea of finding salvation through sin, however shocking this might be to accepted morality. Yet perhaps with the one exception of the play, *Die Wölfe* (The Wolves [1921]), he never found himself in accord with the taste of the theater public. This one play, however, is not only very effective dramatically: it is also a perfect key to his main dramatic intentions.

*The Wolves* (one of three one-acters around the figure of Tolkening) is apparently perfectly normal in language and dramatic form.[39] But the theme of the rather saintly country pastor with a completely demonic country wife is one of extreme violence. The play develops into an open conflict between the spirit and the flesh, a massive assault on life-denying Christianity and a demonstration by the woman of a longing for fulfillment in LIFE which goes far beyond the bounds of normal society. The play closes with a nightmare vision of the demonic woman who has cried: "Oh to be raped to death by a wolf!" heading for her bedroom with her great red beast. Horrible noises are then heard, and her naked body is afterward found on the bed with the throat ripped open.

But despite first appearances, this play is no naturalistic drama of domestic interior in lonely East Prussia. From the start, the tempo is very slow and brooding. Tolkening is haunted by dreams. His newly arrived friend, Dr. Joy, is not the stock "rescuer from afar" of the Naturalist drama but the Expressionist who pierces through surface reality to the heart of the matter and knows "there is more going on than the eye can see." Like the castle in Kafka's only play, *Der Gruftwächter* (The Guardian of the Tomb [1916]), Tolkening's house, with its light shining out into the surrounding darkness, is on the borderland.[40] The people of the village look up to the light, but behind the village stand the dark forests that stretch right through to Russia, even as far as Siberia: "you can feel the great heart of Asia pulsing in your veins." In the same way that the vast primeval forests are let into this one room, so too Dr. Joy makes everyone aware of the vastness of time. It is he, too, who develops the theory of the battle of the sexes that has been going on since the beginning of time, although Anita seems to have arrived at similar conclusions for herself. But in the end what really happens? Is it not all in the mind, a nightmare of the sex-starved Agatha exhausted by long travel, unusual surroundings, and the threatening roar of the ice breaking which punctuates her dreams?

## IX  *Arnolt Bronnen*

Jahnn and Brust might be thought to have reached the ultimate limits of what was acceptable to the theater public, but in fact they were marginal figures, both in a geographical and in a literary sense; and however much critics may reappraise their works and acclaim their virtues as dramatists, they were never at the center of things in their own time. By contrast, Arnolt Bronnen (1895–1959) was from the commencement of his literary career always in the public eye, always capable not only of splitting the critics, but also of producing a scandal at regular intervals.[41] Yet perhaps his greatest quality, one he shares with his contemporaries—Becher, Benn, and Brecht—was his capacity for survival; and so his literary career stretches from the First World War and the succeeding Weimar Republic through the Hitler régime to the German Democratic Republic. His ability to adapt to the prevailing sociopolitical climate makes him a figure of the greatest literary and sociological significance.

Born in 1895 in Vienna, his earlier years were marked by the conflict between himself and his father, whom he always contemptuously referred to as "the Professor." He volunteered for service at the outbreak of hostilities, served from 1914 till 1917, was wounded and ended the war as a prisoner-of-war in Italy where he started to write. After the war he worked in Wertheim's department store in Berlin and with his monocle and tailcoat stood out as something of a Sternheim-style dandy figure in the bohemian circles of the time. His early plays, *Die Geburt der Jugend* (Birth of Youth) and *Vatermord* (Patricide) were probably written about the time of Hasenclever's *The Son* (1915), but they did not appear in print until 1920. *Patricide*, first performed in 1922, was responsible for the first of many

scandals associated with his name. Others were to follow, not
least with *Exzesse* (Excesses [1923]), a comedy in sixteen
scenes, which in its tenth scene has Hildegard lying in the
grass, appealing to a goat:

Komm du Bock komm komm. Ich schrei über die ganze Welt komm
komm. Ich zittere wie ich sein werd und weiss von Orgien und fühl
das Surren meines weissen tollen Leibes. Ach ich bin voll komm
komm. (*Der Bock beschnuppert sie.*) Ich bin Gras du kannst mich
fressen du. Riechst du mich kost mich doch. Wenigstens schlecken
kannst du mich.

(Come on ram come come. I'm screaming throughout the whole
world come come. I'm shaking at what I'll be like when I know
about orgies and feel the humming of my white mad body. Oh, I'm
full come come. (*The ram sniffs her.*) I'm grass you can eat me.
Smell me taste me. At the very least you can lick me.)[42]

*Anarchie in Sillian* (Anarchy in Sillian [1924]) and *Rheinische
Rebellion* (Rebellion on the Rhine [1925]) provided similar
sensations.

As has been seen in connection with the production of Jahnn's
*Pastor Ephraim Magnus,* Bronnen was close to Brecht in the
1920's. However, he moved further and further in the direction
of right-wing politics and became a Nazi (in Tucholsky's words
"a failed left-winger, disguised as a fascist"). About this time
Bronnen worked for radio, became one of the first writers of
radio plays, and was in at the beginnings of television. However, a man of his temperament was liable never to be viewed
with anything other than suspicion in Nazi circles, and he was
banned, declared politically unreliable, and refused permission
to publish. Yet he survived the Nazi period somehow and toward
the end of the war made contact with the Austrian resistance
movement. By the 1950's he was a Communist, which made life
uncomfortable for him in Austria, and so, in 1955, he accepted
Johannes R. Becher's invitation to settle in East Berlin as a
literary critic. He died in an East Berlin hospital in 1959.

With such a checkered career it is little wonder that a great
deal of doubt had been cast on Bronnen's character and hence
on his oeuvre, but there is no doubting the dramatic talent he

displayed in his earlier works, especially *Patricide*. This is far more than just a scandalous work or a theatrical sensation: it is still as powerful today as it was when first written sixty years ago. There are various possible explanations for this fact, not least of which is that Bronnen's play is admirably concentrated. All the action takes place in a tiny flat, occupied by the Fessel family and two female lodgers, in the space of three and a half hours. The time of year is the end of March and the föhn wind is blowing, so already at the start of the play, which is redolent with the sexual stirrings of puberty, there are echoes of Wedekind's *Spring's Awakening*. At first sight the setting suggests a Naturalistic play, and Bronnen's language, too, seems naturalistically down-to-earth, demotic, and apparently far removed from the ecstatic pathos associated with Expressionism. But this is Expressionism nevertheless and not Naturalism: "In the lapidary dramatic style of this drama Bronnen reduces everything to one single conflict: the father oppresses the Son, the Son revolts. The plot is basic: there is an open battle between the two; the Son stabs the Father and thereby achieves the freedom he longs for, at least for a moment of time, and in his imagination."[43] In other words, here again we are faced with the fundamental father-son conflict of the Expressionist generation. Yet as presented by Bronnen, this conflict seems not only possible or even probable but inevitable. The situation becomes a microcosm of the battle being waged in the society of the time.

This revolution is also a sexual revolution, and Bronnen has no hesitation about breaking down taboos. After the first scene, ironically headed "The Brothers," because it shows how hateful brothers can be to each other, comes a scene entitled "The Friends," which introduces Edmund, Walter's rich young friend with anarchist leanings, and "perverse" homoerotic tendencies, who has come to "ruin" him. They are caught by the mother fondling each other.

Yet it is interesting, in view of Bronnen's later association with the National Socialists, that Walter wishes to escape from the decadence of the city to the purity of the land. His father wants him to be a lawyer, but Walter wants to be a farmer, and his language anticipates that of Blut und Boden (Blood and Soil). The scenes that follow are called "The Father," "The

Mother," "The Family," "Refugees," and "The Son." Walter's friend Edmund has already suggested that Walter is in love with his own mother, and this Oedipus theme is developed with mounting tension, first in the Father scene, then in the sexually ambivalent Mother scene, through the other scenes until the very last scene which ends with the triumph of the son.

*Both are excited as possible; she drops the nightdress she has been merely holding in place and stands naked before him. They look at each other until she takes fright and runs away. Walter after her. They run into the next room, where she turns round. Mr. Fessel can meanwhile be heard snorting outside, then talking and opening doors.*
FRAU FESSEL: Aa a ahh—
WALTER:        You—
*Fessel bangs open the window with a meat hammer, revolver in his hand, aims, but is shaking too much; so he comes all the way in, panting, holding his heart, and incapable of uttering a sound. Meanwhile Walter leaps up with his back to him, so that he is standing right in front of his father but cannot see him. Fessel tries to do everything at once, smash, kick, strangle; he shoots and misses, loses the hammer.*
WALTER: (*leaps away, screaming wildly, then without thinking, naked and unarmed, goes for him.*) Now—
*Fessel falls to the ground, the window closes, he tries to shoot.*
WALTER: He's still alive, a — a — a — live, (*roars, gropes for the knife, seizes it, stabs repeatedly at his father, who, filled with rage and hatred, but in weakened condition, has got up and tried to shoot, he dies without getting his breath back. Walter collapses beside him.*[44]

It must be admitted that this is ludicrous, and at least one critic has suggested that the whole play needs to be treated as a tragicomedy. But Bronnen himself was aware of this short-coming, and it is his own irony and lack of elevated pathos which saves him from the worst excesses of the Expressionistic rhetorical tone. On the one hand he seems merely the last in the long line of Expressionists from Kokoschka, through Stramm, Brust, and H. H. Jahnn, who proclaimed salvation through the emancipation of the flesh; on the other he did it in such a way that Brecht, who was normally repelled by Expressionistic pathos, was eager to produce the play. Some critics at the time did see Bronnen as a sexual maniac expressing through his character Walter his own crazed desires, but they had not paid enough attention to the final words of the play, in which Walter rejects his mother and soars heavenward.

> Himmel, ich spring dir auf, ich flieg.
> Es drängt, zittert, stöhnt, klagt, muss auf, schwillt,
> quillt, sprengt, fliegt, muss auf, muss auf,
> Ich,
> Ich blühe —

> Heaven I leap upwards towards you, I fly,
> Something is pressing, shaking, groaning, moaning,
> Must open and swell, pour, burst, fly,
> Must open, must open,
> I
> I'm opening like a flower —

Although throughout there is no mention of religion, such ecstatic longings make this a play which must be seen alongside similar religious works by Barlach, Brust, and H. H. Jahnn.

# CHAPTER 7

## Conclusion

B Y the advent of the Second World War, Expressionism had been almost completely forgotten. By the end of the war, it was evident just how effective the Nazi *Gleichschaltung* had been in erasing Expressionism from the records. Although no one *knew* any more what it was exactly, Expressionism was still generally dismissed as something unpleasant. This was reinforced if anything by the total rejection of Expressionism by influential Marxist critics, such as Lukács, for whom the whole movement had been compounded of unrealistic, formalistic utopianism culminating in fascists like Johst and Benn. Generally speaking, Expressionism had disappeared almost completely, and there seemed to be no modern movement comparable with developments outside Germany. There was, for example, no modern drama, though the meteoric rise of Wolfgang Borchert, who had steeped himself in the theater of the Expressionists, might have directed his public back to the 1920's. But first Germany, which had been hermetically sealed off from the world, had to digest all that was new from England and America.

Thinking of the postwar success in Germany of playwrights like Arthur Miller and Thornton Wilder, Ludwig Marcuse was led to state: "The theater public in Germany got (German) Expressionism second-hand and from abroad."[1] However, there were still some first-hand reminders of the 1920's around; Brecht had come back to his old theater in Berlin; Gottfried Benn, the unreconstructed Expressionist, was also there, ready to make his famous comeback. Memories of the roaring twenties and earlier Expressionism had begun to stir. But Expressionism as such was at first viewed primarily as an *Anregung*, a point of departure for writers since recognized as great, like Benn, Musil, Kafka, Barlach, Brecht. This was not a very fair way to discuss

168

any movement. It was akin to saying (as Soergel did) that Expressionism was to be compared with *Sturm und Drang*, which was important only for its influence on Goethe, Schiller, and Herder. It was not the best approach, but at least research into the early years of the greatest figures of twentieth-century German literature did lead interest back to the sources whence they came, so that critics and historians were forced to ask *Was war Expressionismus?* Fritz Martini brought out a book with this title in 1948, so the vital question was being asked then already. But his little book was only a survey of lost property and dealt mainly with lyric poetry. It did not answer the question, but it did help to initiate an Expressionist revival.

What research since then has established is that the Expressionist period was not only a great age of lyric poetry: it was also a golden age of the theater. Georg Kaiser, Toller, Kokoschka, Sorge, Unruh, Hasenclever, Goering, Barlach, Hans Henny Jahnn have all been made available in modern editions; and in Barlach and Jahnn at least there are reputations which are steadily growing. Sternheim, so long rejected as a cynic without warmth or love, an un-German exponent of grotesque satire in a cold, unnatural mannered style, has been enjoying a renaissance. Satire has become very fashionable, of course, in the second half of the century, but Sternheim has been pleasing not only the fashion-conscious public, but also the academics, an unheard-of combination in Germany. He has become a classic, lavishly edited for West Germany with a special version appearing simultaneously under license in East Germany.

Yet, with Expressionist drama there are still certain problems. Sternheim's comedies are brilliant; Kaiser's *From Morn till Midnight* is a masterpiece; but where is the Shakespeare, the Goethe, or even the Gerhart Hauptmann of the movement? One answer has been given by Hans Schwerte in his discussion of Kokoschka's plays.[2] Schwerte makes the point that such plays cannot be read as *literature*. According to him, Expressionist drama was at its best when at its most *theatrical* and at its least literary, in the same way perhaps that Expressionist poetry was often at its best when it was not *Buchlyrik* but poetry for public performance in cabarets. But even granting this, it would be foolish not to admit that much of Expressionist drama is dated. Nothing dates more quickly than an avant-garde movement; and contemporary political pieces, passionate but youthful outbursts, excessive linguistic experiments, Baroque wordy effusions, have not much appeal for a modern generation, which is said to be too skeptical for O-Mensch Pathos, or for utopian demands for a total renewal of mankind.

The revival of interest in Expressionism has revealed, however, how much of an oversimplification it is to think of Expressionism as first and foremost the chaotic, eruptive, explosive scream. Certainly, as Sokel reminds us, this is a feature of it which can never be ignored: "Many Expressionists endeavored to give the same effect on the printed page that Munch achieved in his painting ["The Scream"]. Some writers expressed their feeling of gruesome urgency through monosyllabic outcries, furious hyperboles, and canonades of exclamation points." But, as Sokel shows, the opposite is also true: "Others, like Kafka with his calmly controlled nightmares or Kaiser with his dagger-thrust dialogues, expressed the same feeling with infinitely greater artistic effectiveness."[3] It is becoming manifestly clear that the Expressionists were by no means all pathos and rhetoric. They could be just as skeptical and critical as the modern generation. Expressionism was not merely unrealistic: it distorted reality in the direction of the grotesque for which the modern generation has discovered such an affinity. As much as anything else, it is probably this cold, hard, satiric, absurd, parodying strain in Expressionism which makes much of it so relevant to the present day.[4]

In any event, a process of revaluation is going on, and already the greatness of Lasker-Schüler, Kaiser, Sternheim, Barlach, and others is being recognized. How far, however, has this process of revaluation extended beyond the boundaries of the German-speaking lands to England and America? Here the problem is complicated by the fact that remarkably little of the immense theatrical activity of the time ever penetrated to the English-speaking world in direct translation. Hence, the impact of Germany's theatrical revolution was, of necessity, for long based on a knowledge of very few dramatists and a very restricted number of plays. Surprisingly, Stramm was translated into English as early as 1914 but seems to have gone completely unnoticed;[5] otherwise the dramatists known outside Germany were Toller, Kaiser, Werfel, and possibly Sternheim.

Unfortunately, too, Expressionism first reached England shortly after 1918, and as a result almost inevitably became associated with a certain leanness and starkness far removed from the startlingly theatrical (and often very expensive) effects demanded by the original German plays. Nevertheless, even on this drastically reduced scale the power of a play like *From Morn till Midnight* was enormous, and the Ashley Dukes' version was brought back again and again. Because of Ashley Dukes' efforts and mainly because of this one play, interest in German Expressionism grew until it eventually became a force to be reckoned with. But it would be an exaggeration to claim that what was happening in one or two little theaters could seriously affect the course of English theater at that time. It was only in the later 1920's and 1930's when Expressionism began to arrive in England from America in the form of plays like Elmer Rice's *The Adding Machine* that the real discussion (and condemnation) of Expressionism began in England and James Agate could write his "Case Against Expressionism."[6]

Ashley Dukes' version of *From Morn till Midnight* was certainly in at the beginning of American interest in theatrical Expressionism. The first American production of the play using his translation was the Theater Guild's from May 21 to August 3, 1922, "the closest Kaiser ever came to a Broadway success." The critical response to the play ran the full gamut from total bewilderment and rejection to unstinted praise. The terms of the bewilderment are conventional and predictable; the words of praise and wonder in *The Dial* (1922) deserve to be quoted at least in part:

Something akin to divine assurance was restored to our theater when *From Morn to Midnight* was produced by the Theater Guild. The certainty we had so long lacked that the theater could give us anything hard and clear, swift and certain in its movement, had been insufficiently challenged in the last year or two; among Americans Mr. O'Neill alone made it advisable to wait and see. We understand fully that *From Morn to Midnight* is neither the best example of Georg Kaiser's work nor an exceptional example of Expressionism on the stage. It is easy to quarrel with the occasional wearing thin of material out of which the play is made. But one cannot question the profound conviction that this play is a way of revelation for the cluttered and floundering theater of our time.[7]

So by reference to Ashley Dukes it can be shown in the English-speaking world there was some interest in theatrical circles in productions of German Expressionist drama. As has been recently shown, however, this interest was out of all proportion to its impact on English playwrights who have always been quick and eager to prove that any similarity between any of their works and German Expressionism can only have been accidental.[8] T. S. Eliot's *Samson Agonistes* may have been described as "a piece of pure Expressionism both in form and content," but Eliot himself preferred to relate the stylization in the play to Noh drama, Ezra Pound, and Yeats. Similarly, even Auden and Isherwood, who have often been thought to have written *The Dog Beneath the Skin* (1935), *The Ascent of F6* (1938), and *On the Frontier* (1939) under the German influence, much preferred references to non-German sources of influence like Shaw, Cocteau, Eliot, and the English Christmas pantomime. Even "the extent and origin of the Expressionist influence in the dramas of Sean O'Casey" has so far not yet been resolved, though O'Neill seems to be emerging as the most likely (indirect) candidate.

If one looks at America in the 1920's, however, the situation is quite different. For the American poets and storytellers the image of Paris still persisted as a "laboratory of the spirit," but the revelance of German Expressionism for the American theater was early recognized. Frederick H. Hofmann, writing on the 1920's, summed up the situation with these words: "Whatever the actual contribution of Expressionism to the American spirit, there is no doubt that it encouraged a remarkable variety of experiments, large and small, on the American stage."[9]

That there was in fact such a range of theatrical experimentation has been shown in detail by Mardi Valgemae in her book, *Accelerated Grimace: Expressionism in the American Drama of the 1920's*. American dramatists and men of the theater were not ashamed to acknowledge their indebtedness to the avant-garde work of German Expressionists. Even before O'Neill there were many experiments in America, yet it is his work that has drawn the attention of critics. Inevitably, *The Emperor Jones* has been compared with Kaiser's *From Morn till Midnight*, *The Hairy Ape* with *The Cabinet of Dr. Caligari*, while *The Great God Brown* features the Expressionistic double or split personality as in Kaiser's *The Coral*. Just as Ashley Dukes is associated with the Little Theater movement in England, so too O'Neill had a number of his plays performed by the Theater Guild and fortunately also had at hand the Provincetown Players, "who provided him and other native playwrights with a laboratory in which to experiment with new dramatic techniques."[10] Expressionist elements can also be found in the dramatic works of Dos Passos, Clifford Odets, and, according to Mardi Valgemae, also in Arthur Miller, Tennessee Williams, Albee, and the new American drama of the 1960's. Valgemae concludes:

Most serious American playwrights as well as many scene designers and directors since the 1920's have grasped the imaginative tools of Expressionism, in order to expose the soul by hacking through what O'Neill called "the banality of surfaces." Numerically American Expressionism was not overwhelming. It is significant, however, that the leading playwrights from O'Neill to Albee and beyond have utilised the Expressionist mode, while verse drama, or what Cocteau called "poetry in the theatre," has all but disappeared from the Modern American stage, a different kind of poetry of the theatre has taken its place. Similarly, such well-known scene designers and directors as Robert Edmond Jones, Throckmorton, Simonson, Kazan, Mielziner, and Ball have assimilated the new mode into their work. Utilizing Expressionist techniques, imaginative writers and scenic artists have created a ritualistic poetry of visual stage metaphors and rhythms that reveals the essence of the human predicament. By dramatizing the tortured inner life of twentieth-century man, American Expressionism has added to the modern repertory a significant body of vivid and dynamic plays.[11]

# Notes and References

## Chapter One

1. John Gassner, "Strindberg the Expressionist," in *August Strindberg: Eight Expressionist Plays* (New York, 1965).
2. See Mathilde Hain, *Studien über das Wesen des frühexpressionistischen Dramas* (Frankfurt/Main, 1933), pp. 12–20. All of Strindberg's plays were available in translation by 1912. At first his naturalistic dramas were performed in Germany, then round the turn of the century the historical and dream plays. After 1913 there was general talk of a "Strindberg cult" and a "Strindberg craze." His plays were particularly popular during the war. Reinhardt alone put on seventeen of them and *To Damascus* became known as "the original breeding cell of Expressionist drama" following Julius Bab's reviews.
3. Lee Simonson, "The Ideas of Adolphe Appia," in Eric Bentley ed., *The Theory of the Modern Stage* (Baltimore, 1969), p. 29.
4. *Ibid.*, pp. 47–48.
5. Quoted from James Roose-Evans, *Experimental Theater, From Stanislavsky to Today* (New York, 1971). See Chapter 7, "Craig and Appia = visionaries," p. 62. See also "Gordon Craigs englische Anfänge und seine Weltwirkung," in Heinz Kindermann, *Theatergeschichte Europas* IX (Salzburg, 1970), pp. 419–55.
6. Heinz Greul, *Bretter, die die Welt bedeuten: Die Kulturgeschichte des Kabaretts* (Munich, 1971), I, 164–65.
7. Quoted from Heinz Greul, *op. cit.*, p. 165.
8. Müllenmeister, quoted by Paul Pörtner, "Expressionismus und Theater," in *Expressionismus als Literatur*, pp. 201–202.
9. "The Epilogue to the Actor," appended to the play *The Seduction* (1913), later developed into the fuller essay "The Man with a Soul and Psychological Man," is available in English in Sokel's *Anthology of German Expressionist Drama*, pp. 6–8.

## Chapter Two

1. Ernst Ribbat, *Die Wahrheit des Lebens im frühen Werk Alfred Döblins* (Münstersche Beiträge zur dt. Literaturwissenschaft vol. 4) (Münster, 1970), 27–28.

2. Louis Huguet, *L'Oeuvre d'Alfred Döblin ou la dialectique de l'exode 1878–1918* (Paris, 1970), Vol. 1/1, pp. 160–92.

3. Joris Duytschaever, "Alfred Döblins Lydia und Mäxchen als Theaterparodie," in *Texte und Kontexte*, Studien zur deutschen und vergleichenden Literaturwissenschaft. Festschrift für Norbert Fuerst zum 65. Geburtstag. Eds. Durzak, Reichmann, and Weisstein (Bern and Munich, 1973), pp. 49–57.

4. Hans Schwerte, "Anfang des expressionistischen Dramas: Oskar Kokoschka," *Zeitschrift für deutsche Philologie*, 83 (1964), 171–89.

5. Horst Denkler, "Die Druckfassungen der Dramen Oskar Kokoschkas," *Deutsche Vierteljahresschrift*, 40 (1966), 94.

6. W. H. Sokel, *An Anthology of German Expressionist Drama*, p. xvii.

7. Hans Schwerte, *op. cit.*, pp. 175–76.

8. Horst Denkler, *op. cit.*, p. 101.

9. Horst Denkler, *Drama des Expressionismus*, pp. 28–36.

10. Richard Sheppard, "Kandinsky's Abstract Drama *Der gelbe Klang*: An Interpretation," *Forum for Modern Language Studies*, 11 (1975), 165–76.

11. Horst Denkler, *Einakter und kleine Dramen des Expressionismus*; p. 278: *"The Yellow Chord*, a sketch for an abstract total work of art and textual basis for a complex stage synthesis, is the only scenario of Kandinsky's to be printed in full. Though never produced during the lifetime of the author, its influence on modern theater cannot be exaggerated. For apart from Hugo Ball and Lothar Schreyer, who directly develop Kandinsky's sketch, other authors and stage people who were not so close to Kandinsky were also inspired by him, to take over this principle of composition, this language of imagery, and this color symbolism or at least to take the possibility of their use seriously."

12. Ingo Wasserka, "Die Sturm— und Kampfbühne, Kunstheorie und szenische Wirklichkeit im expressionistischen Theater Lothar Schreyers," Diss., Vienna, 1965.

13. M. S. Jones, "Art as Necessity; Lothar Schreyer's Concept of Art in 'Der Sturm,' " *German Life and Letters*, 24 (1973), 211.

14. M. S. Jones, *op. cit.*, p. 209; see also Peter Mertz, "Das Bühnenbild der Zwanziger Jahre unseres Jahrhunderts im deutschen Sprachraum," Diss., Vienna, 1959, pp. 118–20.

15. M. S. Jones, *ibid.*, p. 214.

16. Quoted from Julius Bab by F. N. Mennemeier, *Modernes Deutsches Drama I*, 38, the most recent and up-to-date discussion of Stramm, next to Jeremy Adler, "On the Centenary of August

Stramm: An Appreciation of *Geschehen, Rudimentär, Sancta Susanna,* and the 'Abend,' " *Pub. of English Society,* 44 (1973–74), 1–40.

17. J. M. Ritchie, ed., *Seven Expressionist Plays,* pp. 13–14.

18. H. Ihering, "Theater der Expressionisten: Die Sturmbühne im Künstlerhaus," in *Von Reinhardt bis Brecht,* Vol. I, 81.

19. F. N. Mennemeier, *Modernes Deutsches Drama I,* 166–87.

20. "Two Superdramas" by Ivan Goll, tr. W. H. Sokel, *An Anthology of German Expressionist Drama,* pp. 10–11.

21. J. M. Ritchie, ed., *Seven Expressionist Plays,* p. 18.

## Chapter Three

1. R. Hinton Thomas, in Samuel and Thomas, *Expressionism in German Life, Literature and the Theatre,* provided the first important discussion of R. J. Sorge's *Der Bettler* and its importance for Expressionism, pp. 19–37. See also his essay in *Modern Language Review,* XXXII, 3 (1937), "Sorge's development towards Expressionism in the years 1908–10."

2. R. Hinton Thomas, *op. cit.,* pp. 24–25.

3. W. H. Sokel, *An Anthology of German Expressionist Drama,* pp. xxx–xxxi.

4. See Heinz Herald in "Aufführungsgeschichte," G. Rühle, *Zeit und Theater, Vom Kaisereich zur Republik 1913–1925,* I, 850–51. The première took place on December 23, 1917, direction by Max Reinhardt, with Ernst Deutsch as the hero. This marked the beginning of the series of Expressionist plays under the title "Das junge Deutschland." The list of productions, taken from Franz Horch's *Die Spielpläne Max Reinhardts* (Munich, 1930), is given in *The Era of German Expressionism,* pp. 356–57.

5. "Aufführungsgeschichte" of *Der Sohn,* in G. Rühle, *op. cit.,* 854–64.

6. Quoted from G. Rühle, *op. cit.,* 862.

7. Report on the play and first ever interpretation by Kurt Pinthus in *Die Schaubühne,* 1914, quoted from Horst Denkler "Walter Hasenclever," in *Rheinische Lebensbilder,* Vol. IV (Düsseldorf, 1970), 261.

8. Quoted from the introduction to *Walter Hasenclever: Gedichte, Dramen, Prosa* (Hamburg, 1963).

9. See G. Rühle, *op. cit.,* 858–59.

10. Friedrich Koffka, "Über das Schauspiel 'Die Wupper,' " *Das junge Deutschland,* 2 (1919), 120–28.

11. Roland H. Wiegenstein, "Ein Skandal und ein Stück," *Frankfurter Hefte,* 14 (1959), 147–50; André Müller, "Auflösung der bürgerlichen Idylle, Die Wupper von Else Lasker-Schüler in Köln," *Theater der Zeit,* 14 (1959), Heft 2, 48–50.

12. Heinz Herald, "Noch ein Wort zur Wupper-Aufführung," *Das junge Deutschland*, 2 (1919), 129–30. This original production took place on April 27, 1919, as a private performance for the Das junge Deutschland club in Berlin, in Max Reinhardt's Deutsches Theater. Heinz Herald directed, the set was by Ernst Stern, and the music was by Friedrich Hollænder, now famous for his film music and songs (e.g., *The Blue Angel*). Staatliches Schauspielhaus in Berlin, in October 1927. This performance was a great success; reviews in Günther Rühle, *Theater für die Republik*, 806–11.

*Chapter Four*

1. See Günther Erken, "Wortführer des politischen Expressionismus," *Handbuch der Gegenwartsliteratur*, pp. 355–60.

2. Schickele's was the first literary work to deal with a World War One problem. The première was in the Neues Theater, Frankfurt, on December 17, 1916, direction Arthur Hellmer; it was also produced in the Kleines Theater, Berlin, March 30, 1917, under the direction of Georg Alfmann. Reviews in Günther Rühle, *Theater für die Republik*, 48–53.

3. Karl Eibl, *Gustav Sack: Paralyse, der Refraktär* (Munich, 1971).

4. H. F. Garten, *Modern German Drama*, 2nd. ed., p. 122 ff.

5. *Ibid.*, p. 126.

6. Alwin Kronacher, *Fritz von Unruh*, with an intro. by Albert Einstein (New York, 1946), p. 22.

7. Judith A. Taylor, "Death as Escape and Rebirth in Fritz von Unruh's *Ein Geschlecht*," *The Germanic Review*, 44 (1969), 111.

8. Judith A. Taylor, *op. cit.*, 115.

9. Julius Bab, "Fritz von Unruh," *Weltbühne*, 14 (1918), 261–62.

10. Otto F. Best, "Rebellion und Ergebung, Reinhold Goerings *Seeschlacht*, als dreifache Demonstration," *Colloquia Germanica*, I (1973), 146.

11. *Das junge Deutschland*, 2, Heft 9 (1919), quoted from *Zeit und Theater*, I, 878. Other reviews in Günther Rühle, *Theater für die Republik*, 112–18.

12. Ulrich Weisstein, "Goering's Seeschlacht, A New Antigone?" *Drama and Theatre*, Vol. 10, No. 1 (1971), 14.

13. For the most recent study, see Miriam Raggam, *Walter Hasenclever Leben und Werk* (Hildesheim, 1973), pp. 66–109.

14. Letter by Hasenclever from Clamart/Seine, October 11, 1929, replying to *Die Scene*. Quoted from Raggam, *op. cit.*, pp. 98–99.

15. H. F. Garten, *op. cit.*, p. 131.

16. *Vision and Aftermath*, p. 145.

17. *Ibid.*, p. 156.

18. Toller's *Hinkemann* and Brecht's *Baal* were both accepted for production by Alwin Kronacher. The *Hinkemann* première was at the Altes Theater, Leipzig, September 19, 1923, under the direction of Paul Wiecke. *Baal* premièred in the same theater on December 8, 1923, under the direction of Alwin Kronacher. As a result, both plays tended to be reviewed and discussed together. Toller's *Hinkemann* in particular was at the center of an enormous scandal, instigated by Nationalist groups who took offense at the theme and its reflections on the ethos of heroism and military bravery. Contemporary reviews in Rühle, *Theater für die Republik*, 486–93.

19. *Vision and Aftermath*, p. 191.

20. *Ibid.*, p. 197.

## Chapter Five

1. Siegfried Melchinger, *Geschichte des politischen Theaters* (Velber, 1971).

2. Helmut Gruber, "The Political-Ethical Mission of German Expressionism," *The German Quarterly*, 40 (1967), 186. See also Eva Kolinsky, *Engagierter Expressionismus: Politik und Literatur zwischen Weltkrieg und Weimarer Republik* (Stuttgart, 1970).

3. Gruber, *op. cit.*, 194.

4. Gruber, *op. cit.*, 198.

5. Ludwig Rubiner, *Die Gewaltlosen* in Karl Otten, ed., *Schrei und Bekenntnis: Expressionistisches Theater*, p. 304.

6. Bio-bibliographical appendix to Kurt Pinthus' anthology, *Menschheitsdämmerung*, quoted in Rühle, *Zeit und Theater*, I, 891. Rubiner edited various documentary volumes on world revolution and with Holitscher and Karlheinz Martin founded the First Proletarian Theater in 1919.

7. *Zeit und Theater*, I, 891, from Rubiner's essay "Der Dichter greift in die Politik" (The poet takes a hand in politics), *Die Aktion*, 1912.

8. Bertolt Brecht. *Gesammelte Werke in 20 Bänden* (Frankfurt/Main, 1967), XV, p. 34. In this notice on "the series in essay-form," *Der dramatische Wille* published by Kiepenheuer, Brecht praises Kaiser's *Hölle, Weg, Erde*, and the "Bänkelsängerlyrik" of Goll's *Possen*. Toller's *Wandlung* is dismissed as "at best newspaper in poetic form. Flat visions, immediately forgettable. Cosmos thin, Man as object, proclamation, instead of Man. Abstracted Man, the singular of mankind. His case rests in weak hands."

9. Rubiner in *Schrei und Bekenntnis*, p. 304.

10. G. Rühle, *Zeit und Theater*, I, 896, refers to Rubiner's review

of Eduard Stucken's *Lanzelot* in *Das Theater*, I, Heft 7 (1909), a journal then edited by Herwarth Walden.

11. Reviews by Ernst Angel in *Die neue Schaubühne*, 2 (1920), 187–88; Richard Elsner, in *Die deutsche Zeitschrift für Freunde dramatischer Kunst*, 3, 4 (1920), 181–82, and Heinrich in *Die Rote Fahne* (1920), reprinted in Manfred Brauneck, ed., *Die Rote Fahne*, *Kritik, Theorie, Feuilleton 1918–1933* (Munich, 1973); discussed in F. W. Knellesen, *Agitation auf der Bühne*, Das Politische Theater der Weimarer Republik (Emsdetten, 1970), pp. 48–49.

12. Reviews and commentary in Günther Rühle, *Theater für die Republik*, 156–64.

13. Maurice Pittock, "Masse-Mensch and the Tragedy of Revolution," *Forum for Modern Language Studies*, 8 (1972), 162.

14. Reviews of the première in Rühle, *Theater für die Republik*, 320–26.

15. Quoted in Alfred Lieder, "Ein Expressionistischer Aussenseiter," *Der Monat*, Heft 161 (February 1962), p. 71.

16. Erwin Piscator, "Der Weg eines proletarischen Theaterleiters," 1931, in: *Schriften 2*, Aufsätze, Reden, Gespräche, ed., Ludwig Hoffmann, Berlin, 1968. Quoted from Horst Denkler "Der Fall Franz Jung," in *Die sogenannten zwanziger Jahre*, p. 97. For the most recent discussions of Franz Jung see F. N. Mennemeier, *Modernes Deutsches Drama*, I, 205–12, and Horst Denkler, "Der Fall Jung," in *Die sogenannten zwanziger Jahre*, 75–108.

17. Franz Jung, *Wie lange noch?* in *Einakter und Kleine Dramen des Expressionismus*, p. 260.

18. *Einakter und Kleine Dramen des Expressionismus*, p. 262.

19. Franz Jung, *Die Kanaker* (Berlin, 1921), Sammlung revolutionärer Bühnenwerke, Vol. II, 7.

20. Quoted by F. Grieger, "Literarische Notizen zum Werk von Franz Jung," *Schlesien*, 4 (1959), 35–38.

21. Very little critical interest has been shown in Becher as an Expressionist dramatist, but Horst Denkler has included *Ikaros* in his anthology *Einakter und Kleine Dramen des Expressionismus* and Arnim Arnold in *Die Literatur des Expressionismus*, has briefly commented on the two versions of *Arbeiter Bauern Soldaten*, on pp. 139–45.

22. J. R. Becher, *Ikaros* in *Einakter und Kleine Dramen des Expressionismus*, p. 191.

23. J. R. Becher, *Einakter und Kleine Dramen*, p. 191.

24. J. R. Becher, "Leitsätze zur Darstellung des 'Deutschen Pfuhls,'" *Dramatische Dichtungen, Gesammelte Werke*, Vol. VIII (Berlin and Weimar, 1970), 155–56.

25. See Friedrich Wolf, "Ein Klassiker des sozialistischen Realismus," in F. N. Mennemeier, *Modernes Deutsches Drama I*, 231–43.
26. Compare Franz Jung's *Saul* (1916) in *Schrei und Bekenntnis*, 692–712.
27. *Era of German Expressionism*, 244–45.

### Chapter Six

1. Christoph Eykmann, *Denk- und Stilformen des Expressionismus* (Munich, 1974) contains essays on both religion and politics in the Expressionist context. For an early treatment along the same lines see Ludwig Marcuse, "Das Expressionistische Drama," in *Weltliteratur der Gegenwart*, Vol. II (1924), especially "Ethos und Metaphysik," 150 ff.
2. The most recent discussion of Lautensack is that by Otto F. Best, "Heinrich Lautensack oder die Säkularisierung des Eros," *Akzente*, 4 (1970), 370–83, reprinted as the postscript to his edition of *Die Pfarrhauskomödie*. This play is also included in *Schrei und Bekenntnis*.
3. Quoted by Wilhelm Lucas Kirstl, *Heinrich Lautensack, Das Verstörte Fest, Gesammelte Werke*, p. 492.
4. *Lautensack, Gesammelte Werke*, p. 495.
5. *Ibid.*, p. 498.
6. Kasimir Edschmid, *Lebendiger Expressionismus* (Munich, 1961), p. 305.
7. Kasimir Edschmid's review of the première in *Vossische Zeitung*, Berlin, December 12, 1917, reprinted in Rühle, *Theater für die Republik*, 95.
8. Act V, scene ii of Paul Kornfeld, *Die Verführung*, Eine Tragödie in 5 Aufzügen (Berlin, 1916); Kraus Reprint, 1973, p. 191.
9. See Wilhelm Steffens, *Expressionistische Dramatik*, Friedrichs Dramatiker des Welttheaters, Band 37 (Velber, 1968), p. 91.
10. W. H. Sokel, *Anthology of German Expressionist Drama*, p. 6.
11. W. H. Sokel, *ibid.*, p. 8.
12. The last words of the epilogue to this five-act tragedy; see Paul Kornfeld. *Himmel und Hölle*, Eine Tragödie in 5 Aufzügen (Berlin, 1919); Kraus Reprint, 1973, p. 116. Also included in *Schrei und Bekenntnis*.
13. Some reviews in Rühle, *Theater für die Republik*, 227–32.
14. For the briefest account of his literary life, see Lore B. Foltin, *Franz Werfel* (Stuttgart, 1972), which also has full bibliographical information.
15. See Henry A. Lea, "The Failure of Political Activism in Werfel's Plays," *Symposium*, 21 (1967), 330: "In this important state-

ment Werfel rejects activism as an attempt to reform society from without, rather than transforming the individual from within. Believing that regeneration of the individual must precede the regeneration of society, he favours Christianity as the only doctrine demanding ceaseless self-scrutiny of the individual." For literature on the ensuing debate over "The Christian Mission," Lore B. Foltin, *op. cit.*, p. 37.

16. *Schrei und Bekenntnis*, pp. 630–31.

17. For reviews and critical literature on Werfel's *Trojan Women* see Lore B. Foltin, *op. cit.*, pp. 39–40. Discussion in Karl Guthke, "Der Gott der Enttäuschten im deutschen Expressionismus," in *Mythologie der entgötterten Welt* (Göttingen, 1971), pp. 290–313.

18. Quoted in Lore B. Foltin, *op. cit.*, p. 48.

19. A brief account of the critical reception and Kafka's reactions in Lore B. Foltin, *op cit.*, pp. 49–52.

20. For *Spiegelmensch*, see particularly Helga Meister, "Franz Werfels Dramen und ihre Inszenierungen auf der deutschsprachigen Bühne," Diss., Cologne (1964), pp. 24–43, and Paul Wimmer, *Franz Werfels dramatische Sendung*, Profile Band L. (Vienna, 1973), 72–82.

21. In a letter from Werfel to his publisher Kurt Wolff, quoted by Adolf D. Klarmann, *Dramen I*, p. 549 ff.

22. Lore B. Foltin, *op. cit.*, p. 44.

23. For literature on the Kraus-Werfel feud, see Lore B. Foltin, *op. cit.*, pp. 37–38. Most recently Roger Bauer, "Kraus contra Werfel: eine nicht nur literarische Fehde," in *Sprache und Bekenntnis*. Hermann Kunisch zum 70. Geburtstag, 1971, pp. 315–34.

24. J. M. Ritchie, "Translations of the German Expressionists in Eugene Jolas' *transition*," *Oxford German Studies*, 8 (1973), 149–58.

25. *Nuronihar, Eine Pantomime, Aktion 4*, No. 10, März 1914, Sp. 216–18; and in *Carl Einstein, Werke*, pp. 242–55.

26. Some of the twenty scenes that make up *Die schlimme Botschaft* are included in *Schrei und Bekenntnis*. This quotation is from the scene "Die fünf Nägel," in *Carl Einstein, Werke*, p. 391.

27. *Carl Einstein, Werke*, p. 403.

28. Heinz Pollack, "Gotteslästerung-Prozess," *Weltbühne*, 18, Heft 2 (1922), 405–406. See also Kurt Pinthus, "Gotteslästerung," *Das Tagebuch*, Jahrgang III, Heft 42 (1922), 1475–78.

29. Walter Muschg, ed., *Dramen I* (Frankfurt/Main, 1963), Nachwort p. 743.

30. *Ibid.*, p. 744 f.

31. Joachim Schondorff, *Deutsches Theater des Expressionismus* (Munich, 1961). On Hans Rothe's production of *Richard II* see

*Era of Expressionism,* pp. 236–37 and Rühle, *Theater für die Republik,* 350–53.

32. *Medea* is included with commentary in G. Rühle, *Zeit und Theater I* and is available as Reclam Universal-Bibliothek 8711, with commentary by H. L. Arnold; for reviews see *Theater für die Republik,* 710–16. *Schrei und Bekenntnis* has one scene from *Der Arzt, sein Weib und sein Sohn,* which Gustav Gründgens put on at the Hamburg Kammerspiele shortly after its appearance in 1922. Discussion of Jahnn as a dramatist by Edgar Lohner, *Text und Kritik,* H. 2/3 (1964), 4–11, and Georg Hensel, *Spielplan, Schauspielführer,* Teil II (Berlin, 1966), 1177–83.

33. Edgar Gross, "Das preisgekronte Erotomanendrama," *Das literarische Echo,* 23 (1920–21), 968–71. Other reviews in Rühle, *Theater für die Republik,* 469–74.

34. H. Pankow reviewing the Fischer Verlag edition of the text in *Das deutsche Drama,* 4 (1921), 156–57.

35. Julius Bab, "Unterwelt," *Weltbühne* 17, I (1921), 649–53.

36. Edgar Gross, *loc. cit.,* 971.

37. Arnolt Bronnen, *Tage mit Brecht* (Munich, 1960), p. 153. Jahnn commented: "What the public heard and saw, was neither a drama by Jahnn, nor by Brecht—and it wasn't by Bronnen either." Quoted in Rühle, *Theater für die Republik,* 470.

38. Brust is discussed by F. N. Mennemeier, *Modernes Deutches Drama I* in the chapter "Ex oriente lux! Alfred Brust," 27–35, while Horst Denkler has recently edited a good selection of his dramas with commentary.

39. See *Seven Expressionist Plays,* p. 19.

40. Also included in translation in *Seven Expressionist Plays.*

41. Bio-bibliographical information in Edwin Klinger, *Arnolt Bronnen, Werke und Wirkung,* Eine Personalbibliographie (Hildesheim, 1974).

42. *Exzesse* was first performed in 1925 and was a scandalous success. The revival in Wuppertal, 1973, was an equally uproarious success. See Klinger, p. xv.

43. From F. N. Mennemeier's chapter on Bronnen "Zirkel der Unterdrückung," *Modernes Deutsches Drama I,* 65.

44. Quoted from Arnolt Bronnen, *Vatermord,* ed. Artur Müller, Dramen der Zeit, 9 (Emsdetten, 1954), 184–85.

## Chapter Seven

1. Ludwig Marcuse, "Eine Renaissance des deutschen Expressionismus," *German Quarterly,* 23 (1958), p. 115.

2. H. Schwerte, "Anfang des expressionistischen Dramas; Oskar Kokoschka," *Zeitschrift für deutsche Philologie*, 83 (1964), 171–91.

3. W. Sokel, *op. cit.*, p. 14.

4. See Karl Otten, *Expressionismus-Grotesk* (Zürich, 1962).

5. *Poet Lore*, Vol. 25, no. 6 (1914).

6. James Agate, "The Case against Expressionism. *The Adding Machine*: a play by Elmer Rice, Court Theatre, 9 January 1928," in *Their Hour Upon the Stage* (Cambridge, England, 1930), pp. 30–34.

7. *The Dial*, 63 (1922), 116.

8. Breon Mitchell, "Expressionism in English Drama and Prose Literature," in *Expressionism as an International Literary Phenomenon*, pp. 181–92. See also the same author's "W. H. Auden and Christopher Isherwood: The German Influence," *Oxford German Studies*, No. 1 (1966), 163–72.

9. Frederick J. Hofmann, *The Twenties* (New York, 1955), p. 168.

10. Mardi Valgemae, "Expressionism in American Theater," in *Expressionism as an International Literary Phenomenon*, pp. 193–203.

11. *Ibid.*, p. 203.

# Selected Bibliography

PRIMARY SOURCES

1. In English

RITCHIE, JAMES M. (ed.) *Seven Expressionist Plays.* (London: Calder
and Boyars, 1968). Translations of Kokoschka's *Murderer Hope
of Womankind,* Kafka's *Guardian of the Tomb,* Barlach's *Blue
Boll,* Kaiser's *Protagonist,* Stramm's *Awakening,* Brust's *Wolves,*
Goll's *Methusalem.* Useful introduction on the theater of Expressionism.

————. *Vision and Aftermath.* (London: Calder and Boyars, 1969).
Translations of four war plays: Hauptmann's *War,* Goering's
*Naval Encounter,* Hasenclever's *Antigone,* and Toller's *Hinkemann.* Good introduction on the Expressionist treatment of the
war and its aftermath in drama.

————. *Carl Sternheim: Five Plays* (London: Calder and Boyars,
1970). Translations of *The Knickers, The Snob, Schippel, 1913,*
and *The Fossil.* Good introduction on Sternheim's Scenes from
the Heroic Life of the Middle Classes and on comedy in the age
of Expressionism.

————. *Georg Kaiser: Five Plays* (London: Calder and Boyars,
1970). Translations of Kaiser's *From Morn till Midnight, The
Burghers of Calais, The Coral, Gas I,* and *Gas II* with an informative critical introduction on Kaiser's Expressionist period.

SOKEL, WALTER H. (ed.) *An Anthology of German Expressionist
Drama.* A Prelude to the Absurd (Garden City, New York: An-
chor Books, 1963). Translations of Kokoschka's *Murderer,* three
acts of Sorge's *Beggar,* Sternheim's *Strongbox,* Kokoschka's *Job,*
Hasenclever's *Humanity,* Kaiser's *Alkibiades Saved,* Goll's *The
Immortal One,* Lauckner's *Cry in the Street,* and Brecht's *Baal.*
The volume also has important theoretical essays in translation
by Rubiner, Kornfeld, Goll and Kaiser, as well as a stimulating
introduction.

2. In German

DENKLER, HORST (ed.). *Einakter und kleine Dramen des Expressionismus* (Stuttgart: Reclam, 1968). An essential anthology,

which for the first time makes works like Kandinsky's *Yellow Chord* readily available. Also included among its 16 playlets are Döblin's *Lydia and Maxie*, Kokoschka's *Murderer Hope of Womankind*, Benn's *Ithaka*, Becher's *Ikaros*, Brust's *The Indian Play*, and Jung's *How Much Longer?*

OTTEN, KARL (ed.). *Schrei und Bekenntnis* (Darmstadt: Luchterhand, 1959). This collection of texts, which helped to launch the Expressionist revival, contains 36 dramatic pieces from the period of Expressionism. Among them are plays otherwise hard to find like Carl Hauptmann's *War* and Franz Jung's *Saul*.

RÜHLE, GÜNTHER. *Zeit und Theater. Vom Kaiserreich zur Republik 1913–1925* (Berlin: Propylaen Verlag, 1973). An anthology which is invaluable not only for making easily available plays like Rubiner's *Those Without Violence*, Kornfeld's *The Seduction*, von Unruh's *One Family*, Bronnen's *Anarchy in Sillian*, and Jahnn's *Medea*, but also for Günther Rühle's extremely informative commentaries on all 12 plays included.

SCHONDORFF, JOACHIM (ed.). *Deutsches Theater des Expressionismus* (Munich: Langen-Müller, 1961). An orthodox selection of texts apart from Jahnn's *Coronation of Richard III*. The introduction by Paul Pörtner conveys much pertinent information.

NOTE: Good modern collected editions are now readily available for the works of Barlach, Becher, Brust, Einstein, Goering, Goll, Hasenclever, Jahnn, Kaiser, Kokoschka, Lasker-Schüler, Lautensack, Sack, Schickele, Sorge, Sternheim, Stramm, Toller, von Unruh, Werfel, and Wolf. Rather more difficult to obtain are Expressionist plays by Bronnen. Modern anthologies like those listed above have helped make Kornfeld, Rubiner, and Jung more accessible, and Kornfeld's two plays, *Seduction* and *Heaven and Hell*, have also been reprinted by Kraus in 1973, in the Expressionism Reprint Series.

## SECONDARY SOURCES

BAULAND, P. *The Hooded Eagle* (Syracuse University Press, 1968). An excellent account of the impact made by Expressionism on the American stage.

EISNER, LOTTE. *The Haunted Screen* (University of California Press, 1969; London: Thames and Hudson, 1969, and Cinema Two Paperback). Expressionism in the German Cinema and the Influence of Max Reinhardt. Wonderful illustrations and good text, though perhaps too much is made of the roots of Expressionism in German Romanticism.

GARTEN, H. F. *Modern German Drama* (London: Methuen, 1959; University Paperbacks, 1964). Good general coverage of Expressionist drama though now dated in approach.

GRUBER, HELMUT. "The Political and Ethical Mission of German Expressionism," *German Quarterly*, 40 (1967), 186–203.

HILL, CLAUDE and RALPH LEY. *The Drama of German Expressionism* (Chapel Hill: University of North Carolina Press, 1960). The standard German-English bibliography, now in need of updating.

KRACAUER, SIEGFRIED. *From Caligari to Hitler* (Princeton University Press, 1947). The classic history of the German film in the period of Expressionism.

KRISPYN, EGBERT. *Style and Society in German Literary Expressionism* (Gainesville, Fla.: University of Florida Press, 1964). A good brief survey.

PASCAL, ROY. *From Naturalism to Expressionism* (London: Weidenfeld and Nicholson, 1973). An excellent study of the intellectual background to German literature and society 1880–1918.

RAABE, PAUL (ed.) and J. M. RITCHIE (tr.). *The Era of German Expressionism* (London: Calder and Boyars, 1974; Oceanside C.A.: Evergreen, 1974). An excellent collection of essays, memories, and accounts of the turmoils of the time by those contemporaries most directly involved with much bibliographical and background material.

RITCHIE, J. M. "Ashley Dukes and the German Theater between the wars." In *Affinities*, ed. R. Last (London: Oswald Wolff, 1971), 97–109. An essay on the importance of Ashley Dukes who translated German Expressionist drama and successfully produced it in England and America after the First World War.

SAMUEL, R. and R. H. THOMAS. *Expressionism in German Life, Literature and the Theatre (1910–1924)* (Cambridge, England: Heffer, 1939). One of the very first surveys in English and still very valuable.

SOKEL, W. H. *The Writer in Extremis* (Stanford University Press, 1959). A classic study of Expressionism in twentieth-century German literature.

VALGEMAE, MARDI. *Accelerated Grimace* (Carbondale: Southern Illinois University Press, 1972). An important study of Expressionism in the American drama of the 1920s.

WEISSTEIN, ULRICH (ed.). *Expressionism as an International Literary Phenomenon* (Paris: Didier, 1973). A vast and valuable collection containing 21 essays and an extensive bibliography.

WILLETT, JOHN. *Expressionism* (London: Weidenfeld and Nicholson,

1970). A wide-ranging, illustrated account of Expressionism in all its many manifestations.

## 2. In German and French

ARNOLD, ARMIN. *Die Literatur des Expressionismus* (Stuttgart: Kohlhammer, 1966). Useful for its treatment of Walden, Stramm, and the Futurists, as well as for the rare discussion of Becher as a dramatist.

BABLET, DENIS and JEAN JACQUOT (eds.). *L'Expressionisme dans le théâtre européen* (Paris: Editions du Centre Nationale de la Recherche Scientifique, 1971). A useful collection of papers from a symposium held in Strassbourg in 1968.

DENKLER, HORST. *Drama des Expressionismus.* Programm, Spieltext, Theater (Munich: Fink, 1967). The best and most searching study of Expressionist drama, but very difficult reading.

DIEBOLD, BERHARD. *Anarchie im Drama.* Kritik und Darstellung der modernen Dramatik (Berlin-Wilmersdorf: H. Keller, 1928; Reprint London, New York, 1972). One of the first accounts of Expressionist drama in German and still fascinating.

FRIEDMANN, HERMANN and OTTO MANN (eds.). *Expressionismus.* Gestalten einer literarischen Bewegung (Heidelberg: Rothe, 1956). A collection of essays reflecting the post-1945 Expressionist revival. Since superceded in part by Wolfgang Rothe's massive volume.

IHERING, HERBERT. *Von Reinhardt bis Brecht.* Vier Jahrzehnte Theater und Film. 3 vols. (Berlin: Aufbau Verlag, 1958, 1959, 1961). An indispensable collection of reviews covering four decades.

MENNEMEIER, F. N. *Modernes Deutsches Drama I, 1910–1933.* Kritiken und Charakteristiken (Munich: UTB, 1973). The best of recent histories of German drama and the first to treat figures like Stramm, Brust, Jung, and Rubiner seriously as dramatists.

PAULSEN, WOLFGANG. *Expressionismus und Aktivismus.* Eine typologische Untersuchung (Berlin and Leipzig: Gotthelf, 1935). An early classic in the study of German Expressionism.

——— (ed.). *Aspekte des Expressionismus* (Heidelberg: Stiehm, 1968). The papers read at the first Amherst Colloquium on Expressionism.

RISCHBIETER, H. *Bühne und bildende Kunst im xx. Jahrhundert* (Velber bei Hannover: Friedrich, 1968). A very large and very beautiful book, invaluable for its magnificent illustrations of Expressionist stage designs and sets, and for its non-literary theatrical approach.

ROTHE, WOLFGANG (ed.). *Expressionismus als Literatur* (Bern: Francke, 1969). Included in this enormous book are essays on leading Expressionist dramatists.

RÜHLE, GÜNTHER. *Theater für die Republik 1917–1933* (Frankfurt/Main: S. Fischer, 1967 ff.). This volume contains contemporary reviews of most of the Expressionist productions of the period.

SZONDI, PETER. *Theorie des modernen Dramas* (Frankfurt/Main: Suhrkamp, 1956; edition Suhrkamp, 1973). A classic work on the theory of modern drama, including Expressionism.

# Index

191

**DATE DUE**

| | | | |
|---|---|---|---|
| | | | |
| | | | |
| | | | |
| | | | |
| | | | |
| | | | |
| | | | |
| | | | |
| | | | |
| | | | |
| | | | |
| | | | |
| | | | |
| | | | |
| | | | |
| | | | |

DEMCO 38-297